Edmund Burke

Portrait of Edmund Burke
James Northcote (1746-1831)
Royal Albert Memorial Museum, Exeter, UK
Courtesy of Bridgeman Art Library International Ltd., London/New York

Edmund Burke

A Genius Reconsidered

Russell Kirk

with a foreword by
Roger Scruton

Intercollegiate Studies Institute
Wilmington, Delaware
1997

Library of Congress Catalog Cataloging-in-Publication Data

Kirk, Russell, 1918-1994
    Edmund Burke: A Genius Reconsidered/Russell Kirk;
with a foreword by Roger Scruton. —Rev. ed. —Wilmington,
DE : Intercollegiate Studies Institute, 1997.
        p.   cm.
    Includes bibliographical references and index.
    1. Burke, Edmund, 1729-1797—Contributions in
political science. 2. Political science—History—Great Britain. I.
Title.
JC176.B83 K57 1997   97-073139
320/.01—dc21   CIP
ISBN 1-882926-17-x

Published in the United States by:

Intercollegiate Studies Institute
P.O. Box 4431
Wilmington, DE 19807-0431
http:/www.isi.org

Manufactured in the United States of America

Contents

Foreword

Politician, propagandist, philosopher, man of letters—Burke was one of the outstanding figures of the eighteenth century, and the first statesman to recognize that there is no coherent response to the Enlightenment apart from social and political conservatism. It is unlikely that such a man should ascend to political office today. The democratic process prefers the glib, the half-educated and the plausible over the literate and the wise. How different things were when Burke entered the House of Commons readers of Dr. Kirk's biography will discover. The American colonist, the Indian peasant, the French aristocrat—all found an advocate in Parliament who was as cool, eloquent, and profound a philosopher as could be found in any Parisian attic or Oxford common room. Burke could command the floor of the Commons; he could also dominate the opinion of the educated classes. His writings changed the course of politics, and laid the foundation for a political philosophy which has lasted to our day, finding its most powerful modern American representative in Russell Kirk.

It is especially welcome that Kirk's biography should be reissued in this bicentennial year of Burke's death. Intelligence, cunning, know-how, stratagems, policies—all these we have in abundance. But wisdom—that sedate and circumspect awareness of the complexity of human things which we find in both Burke and his biographer—is rare among us. We do not listen to ancestral voices, or strive to hear, beneath the din of politics, the rumors sent down to us from former times, which tell us of our imperfection. And until we listen, our future is in jeopardy.

The life that Kirk describes in these pages was a life of action; but it was an action which both sprang from thought and engendered thought. Perhaps no politician has ever speculated so deeply about the nature and limits of the human psyche as Burke. And his speculations are at every point put to practical use, in order to warn against the crazy desire to overthrow the laws and institutions on which our civilization has been erected. Dr. Kirk took up the mantle of Burke, and wrote passionately and wisely of "permanent things," showing his fellow Americans that they could drift away from the vision of the Founding Fathers only at their peril. He was the conscience of modern America just as Burke was the conscience of Enlightenment Britain. Both understood that politics is possible only if some things remain unquestioned, and only if the desire to improve the world rests from time to time in a consciousness that the future cannot be known.

Kirk was not a politician, but he earned the respect of politicians, and strove to elevate the language and the thought of American conservatism to the level of his great predecessor. He learned from Burke that style is not a decorative adjunct to thought, but belongs to its essence. Because he found the words and the images with which to convey his vision to the youth of America, real conservative politicians continue to emerge in the United States, and to direct the future of their country along the path laid down for it by the contemporaries of Burke.

Kirk's biography tells the story of a remarkable statesman, of a remarkable society, and of a remarkable period of human history. English readers will be gratified by the author's sympathy for our eccentricities, while American readers will learn much about the British Empire and its meaning. The book provides a clear and succinct guide to one of the great conservative thinkers of modern times. Kirk sees his subject as he was, and in terms of hopes and fears which he shares. Burke was engaged, he argues, in a continuous pursuit of justice, and valued order, tradition, and the conservative instinct largely because they prevent the massive injustices which ensue when men take it on themselves to manage their own destiny.

The lessons for us are many, and delicately suggested. Like Burke, Russell Kirk is no tub-thumping moralist, but a quiet, ironical and compassionate observer, who writes with a delightful ease and spontaneity. There is no finer monument to Burke than this book by his most original American disciple.

—Roger Scruton

Prefatory Note

During the past forty years, immensely more has been learnt about Edmund Burke than the nineteenth-century biographers and critics knew. This short critical study, taking advantage of the opening to the public of a mass of Burke's papers, the publication of his correspondence in a scholarly edition, and the appearance of several important specialized accounts of Burke, is an attempt to assess Burke afresh.

Readers wishing to know more about the great statesman and man of letters will do well to turn to Carl B. Cone's thorough and impartial political biography, *Burke and the Nature of Politics* (two volumes, 1957 and 1964); it is five times as long as the present essay in biography. The early life (1824) by James Prior remains worth reading; but most of the other biographies have been superseded by the discovery of new information, are superficial, or are long out of print and rarely encountered.

I heartily commend the scholarly studies about one or another aspect of Burke's mind or career by Ross J. S.

Hoffman, Thomas W. Copeland, Peter Stanlis, Francis Canavan, James T. Boulton, Donald Cross Bryant, Gaetano Vincitorio, Thomas H. D. Mahoney, H. V. F. Somerset, Charles Parkin, Jeffrey Hart, Harvey C. Mansfield, Jr., R. R. Fennessey, Lucy S. Sutherland, John A. Woods, and other writers of recent years. Reference is made to these in the chapter-notes or in the bibliographical note at the end of this volume.

Some small portions of this brief life have been published in *The Kenyon Review, The Sewanee Review,* and *Queen's Quarterly.*

—Russell Kirk
Piety Hill
Mecosta, Michigan

Acknowledgments for Revised Edition

Andrew Shaugnessy, Claudia Pasquantonio, Glenn Pierce, Ellen Fielding, and Brooke Daley assisted in the preparation of this updated and revised volume. The foreword, epilogue, and chronology were added by the editor. Bruce Frohnen and Mark C. Henrie kindly suggested recent Burke scholarship to include in the bibliographical note. The dedication remains in the memory of John Abbot Clark.

—Jeffrey O. Nelson
Intercollegiate Studies Institute

Selected Events in the Life of Edmund Burke

1729   Born in Dublin, January 12.

1741   Educated in Ballitore.

1743-48 Educated at Trinity College, Dublin.

1747   Commences *The Sublime and Beautiful.*

1748   Enters the Middle Temple, London.

1750   Arrives in London to study law.

1756   *A Vindication of Natural Society.*

1757   Marries Jane Nugent.
        The Sublime and Beautiful is published.
        Commences an *Abridgement of English
        History* (not published until 1811).
        Newcastle Ministry.

1758   Birth of Burke's son, Richard.

1759   First *Annual Register* published (Burke
        continues as editor until 1765-66).

1761   Bute Ministry. Spends winters, 1761-62 and 1762-63 in Dublin as Hamilton's assistant. Fragment on *Irish Penal Laws*.

1763   Grenville Ministry.

1763-64   Founds Literary Club with Dr. Johnson and Joshua Reynolds.

1765   First Rockingham Ministry.
Secretary to Lord Rockingham.
Elected to the House of Commons for Wendover.

1766   Burke enters House of Commons.
Chatham Ministry.

1768   Grafton Ministry.
Burke purchases Gregories, estate at Beaconsfield.

1769   *Observations on Present State of Nation.*

1770   *Thoughts on Present Discontents.*
North Ministry.

1771-74   Burke retained as agent for New York.

1772   Opposes clergy petition against subscription.
Speech on Protestant dissenters.

1774   *Speech on American Taxation.*
Elected to House of Commons for Bristol.

1775   *Speech on Conciliation with America.*

1776   *Address to the King.*

1777   *Letters to Sheriffs of Bristol.*

1780   *Speech on Economical Reform.*
       Elected to House of Commons for Malton.

1782   Second Rockingham Ministry.
       Burke becomes Paymaster-General.
       Death of Lord Rockingham.
       Shelburne Ministry.

1783   Fox-North coalition Ministry.
       Speech on Fox's East India Bill.

1784   Pitt Ministry.

1785   *Speech on Nabob of Arcot's Debts.*

1786   Proceedings against Hastings.

1787   Impeachment of Hastings.

1789   French Revolution.

1790   *Reflections on the Revolution in France.*
       Burke-Fox quarrel splits Whig Party.

1791   *Letter to a Member of the National Assembly.*
       Appeal from the New to the Old Whigs.
       Thoughts on French Affairs.

1792   *Remarks on the Policy of the Allies.*

1794   Deaths of Burke's brother and son.
       Burke retires from Parliament.

1795   Hastings acquitted by House of Lords.
       Thoughts and Details on Scarcity.
       Letter to a Noble Lord.

1796   *Letters on a Regicide Peace.*

1797   Burke dies, July 9, at Beaconsfield.

1

How Dead Is Burke?

In College Green, at the gate of Trinity College, near the heart of Dublin, stand the handsome statues of Edmund Burke and Oliver Goldsmith. Though these contemporaries were graduates of Trinity, and very Irish after their fashion, their lives were spent principally in London. "The noblest prospect a Scotchman ever sees is the high road which leads him to England," said Samuel Johnson, a friend to both these Irishmen. This was as true, in the eighteenth century, of the Irish.

In a house—thoughtfully demolished some years ago—on Arran Quay, only a few minutes' walk from Trinity College, Edmund Burke was born on January 12, 1729. He may have been baptized in the medieval church of St. Michan, nearby. Dublin then was rising toward the height of its prosperity and fame, although in Burke's childhood those great Georgian buildings the Four Courts and the Custom House had not yet been erected beside the River Liffey. Charming Georgian Dublin, built mostly in Burke's own lifetime, stood virtually intact until recent years, but now is decayed into a howling slum or is being pulled down by Philistine public authorities and tasteless "improvers." Much else that the reforming conservative loved has gone by the board.

Even though he was the son of a successful lawyer, connected with Irish county families, no one could have expected, in 1729, the eminence which this boy would attain. It was an age of aristocracy, which the Tory statesman and philosopher Bolingbroke hoped would be dominated by men of "aristocratic virtue" influenced by humane learning. Relatively obscure, the Burkes were provincial, and not rich. This boy, it turned out, was a being of genius; yet, as he wrote near the end of his course:

> At every step of my progress in life (for in every step was I traversed and opposed), and at every turnpike I met, I was obliged to shew my passport, and again and again to prove my sole title to the honor of being useful to my country, by a proof that I was not wholly unacquainted with its laws, and the whole system of its interests both abroad and at home. Otherwise no rank, no toleration even, for me.[1]

Like many Irish couples of that time, the elder Burkes had entered into a "mixed marriage," Edmund's father being a member of the Church of Ireland—an Anglican, that is—and his mother a Catholic. With his two brothers, Edmund was reared as an Anglican; while his sister, Juliana, brought up in the "old profession," remained all her life an ardent Catholic. One of Burke's chief endeavors in Parliament, half a century later, was to effect the amendment of the "Penal Laws" that weighed down Irish Catholics. Burke's early career was hampered somewhat by the suspicion of the Whig Duke of Newcastle, and others, that the rising young man was a secret Papist, or even a Jesuit in disguise—and political caricaturists later sometimes draped him in a Jesuit habit.

Despite these impediments, Edmund Burke was to become the most interesting of British political philosophers, one of the greatest of modern rhetoricians, the principal intellectual leader of the Whig party, and the most formidable opponent of the French Revolution and of "armed doctrine" generally. He drew up, in the phrase of Harold Laski, "the permanent manual of political wisdom without which statesmen are as sailors on an uncharted sea."

Burke became a public man. Little mentioned in the many volumes of his letters, his private life is sufficiently obscure, for he labored incessantly as a practical politician, with slight leisure for epistolary pleasantries; also, while very young, he remarked that it is well to tell the world no more of one's self than the world must know. The biographer, therefore, patches together as best he may the fragments which distinguish Burke the man from Burke the leader of party and Burke the philosopher. And it is, after all, the public Burke who matters. This short biography is chiefly an account, then, of a "new man" who by power of intellect and remarkable diligence rose to distinction in his time and to influence long thereafter. Burke's private life—aside from the frustrated schemes of his kinsmen—was exemplary but unexciting; Burke's public life shows us the process by which, through experience of the world and through the life of the mind, an Irish writer and political partisan made of himself one of the wisest men ever to meditate upon the civil social order.

As a practical politician, Burke did not succeed conspicuously. During the larger part of his career, he stood among the opposition—stood grandly, but out of office. In the hour of his death, 1797—"a terrible moment in the history of England and of Europe," as John Morley wrote— he beheld the triumph of his denunciations of the Revolution in France, but only a triumph of dubious battle. The passing of a mere half-century was to bring the *Communist Manifesto*. And from the day of his death onward, historians have recorded the effacing, in much of the world, of that order governed by what Burke described as the spirit of religion, and the spirit of a gentleman.

But Burke was more than a party leader and a man of his time. As the champion of what T. S. Eliot called "the permanent things," Burke did not fail, nor is he archaic. He speaks to our age.

Before the middle of this century, however, Burke was little more than recorded, respected, ignored. John Morley had predicted, in 1888, "It seems probable that he will be more frequently and more seriously referred to within the next twenty years than he has been within the whole of the last eighty."[2] This did not come to pass—not then. Twenty-five years later, Paul Elmer More stated that Morley had been in error;[3] and not until 1949 was a revival of strong interest in Burke discernible.

In that year, a scholar of German upbringing remarked to this writer that among educated men in the United States existed a curious ignorance of Burke—who, with his power of style, the varied aspects of his genius, and the breadth of his intellect, might be supposed to attract the attention of those circles that pride themselves upon their grasp of modern thought; and my German friend attributed this condition to a vague popular impression that Burke "had been wrong about France" and somehow was not quite the reading for a liberal. Just then, "liberal" was the word for conjurers in the American groves of Academe.

Yet by 1950, Mr. Lionel Trilling expressed doubts of the efficacy of liberal concepts, and Mr. Arthur M. Schlesinger, Jr., confessed, "We find Burke more satisfying today than Paine, Hamilton or Adams than Jefferson, Calhoun than Clay or Webster." Since then, Burke has been re-discovered. A score of scholarly studies, some of them specialized, have dealt with him. Popularly, and by politicians, he is mentioned and quoted more frequently than he had been in all the interval since 1832. We are even told of an eccentric in the Bowery passing out cards with the legend "Burke saves."

The rising generation, to which Burke appealed at the conclusion of his prosecution of Warren Hastings, has found him anew. Prejudice, interest, and conscience have informed much of the American public that Burke should be read; his name is known again in Europe, too, and even in Africa. The young people who browse in bookshops look for Burke now; and even American and English professors admit that he is of an interest more than antiquarian.

Paradoxically, the resurrection of Burke is a product of modern discontents. Uncertain of the dogmas of liberalism (which Santayana knew for a mere transitory phase), disillusioned with Giant Ideology, the modern serious public is willing to give Burke a hearing. Burke's ideas interest nearly anyone nowadays, including men bitterly dissenting from his conclusions. If conservatives would know what they defend, Burke is their touchstone; and if radicals wish to test the temper of their opposition, they should turn to Burke. Having done this, some conservatives may find that their previous footing was insecure; while some radicals may acknowledge that the position of traditionalists is tenable, or that Burke, too, was a liberal—if liberalism be in any degree associated with ordered freedom.

At a New York club, about 1913, Paul Elmer More happened to mention Burke's name; and a companion inquired, "Burke? He's dead, is he not?" In spirit, Burke is stirring once more. Some there are who wish Burke were immured forever in his tomb. Some years ago, a British scholar professed his sorrow that, in America today, "Burke is being used for political purposes." This gentleman would prefer to keep Burke as a kind of cadaver, out of which doctoral dissertations might be carved. (Burke himself, one may remark, would have been amused and vexed at the notion that a dead master of politics never should influence the living: as statesman and as rhetorician, he intended his speeches and writings for immediate *use*—and for use by the rising generation and by posterity, if useful they might be found. The closet theoretician, the abstract metaphysician, the "drydocked" scholar, Burke cordially detested.)

Burke expected to be disinterred—though not, perhaps, after the fashion in which he has been raised up in the latter half of the twentieth century. Fearing that triumphant Jacobins would treat his corpse as Cromwell's had been dishonored at the Restoration—that his head and limbs might be impaled on some Temple Bar—he left instruction for his body to be buried secretly, somewhere in Beaconsfield church or churchyard, and to this day no man knows the precise spot where Burke lies.

Yet Burke has been invoked in all honor, because he is one of those giants who (in the phrase of the medieval Schoolmen) support us upon their shoulders, one of those dead who walk. Burke endures as part of a great continuity and essence. He offers an alternative to the dreary doctrines of ideology in the mass age.

During the era from Burke's last years to our rough hour, the kaleidoscope of history has suffered a catastrophic spin. A decade before *Reflections on the Revolution in France* came from the press, American troops at Yorktown had greeted Cornwallis with the tune of "The World Turned Upside Down"; and that air, mingling now and then with the "Carmagnole," has been blaring ever since. The stern vaticinations of Burke, which seemed to most nineteenth-century liberals the follies of a deranged old genius, have come to pass: the gods of the copybook headings with terror and slaughter return. Nations dissolving into mere aggregations of individuals, under squalid oligarchs; property reapportion by arbitrary political power; great states ground into powder; the rise of a leveling frenzy—Communism—fierce enough to affright Jacobins; wars far more ruinous than those of the eighteenth century, so that often civilization seems on the brink of dissolution: where has been the divine guidance Burke discerned in history? Perhaps it could have been understood as the punishment of disobedience: "The Lord made all things for Himself—yea, even the wicked for the day of evil."

Our age has experienced the disintegration of the notion of irresistible social progress—vanished in a vortex of atomic waste. "It's not a question of whether you believe Communism is right," an acquaintance of mine used to say, "it's simply that you have to go along with the stream." But after this quasi-Hegelian dictum he would hesitate oddly, as if some doubt had crept in—perhaps the reflection that "even the weariest river winds"—why, to the great deep. If the "Progress" of the Enlighteners has led to a precipice above a silent sea—and such quavers as my friend's have become more frequent—it may be time to conserve, rather than to covet. Against the overweening self-confidence of modern man, Burke contended. If ever we are to learn from the past, today we must descend, Ulysses-like, to interrogate the shades; otherwise we may be numbered among them. Burke may be our Tiresias.

Burke was essentially a modern man, and his concern was with our modern perplexities. "The gift of prophecy," a reviewer for the *Times Literary Supplement* remarked some time ago, "Burke possessed in abundance."

Yet no one speaks of an Age of Burke. In literature, we call Burke's period the Age of Johnson; in philosophy and politics, we might call it the Age of Rousseau.

The Age of Rousseau: the era of abstraction, feeling, emancipation, expansion, equality, the people absolute, the kiss bestowed upon the universe, the deity impotent. The system of Burke: prescription, experience, duty, old ties, social gradation, the reign of law, the love engendered by association, the Author of our being omnipotent. Rousseau and Burke stand at the antipodes, despite the curious theory of some writers that they are two peas in a libertarian pod. Though Rousseau cannot be credited, like Burke, with the foundation almost single-handed of a body of political belief, still the movement of which he was the most influential representative can claim the fealty of several devotees for every one of Burke's, perhaps: the romantic gaze of Jean Jacques darts out, at intervals, from behind a variety of masks—the flushed face of Paine, the grim brow of Marx, the pedantic countenance of John Dewey. Indeed, the disciples of Burke himself, in the generation after his death, were the heirs of Rousseau as well—Coleridge, Southey, Wordsworth. Let us concede that a knowledge of the mind of Rousseau is as important as an apprehension of Burke's, for any man who would understand our present discontents. Admit this, and ask what other thinker, in Burke's lifetime, equaled him in importance.

Foreseeing a sack of the world by the forces of Chaos and old Night, Burke endeavored to save the best of the traditional order within the barricades of institution and philosophy. He was the first conservative of our time of troubles. He labored to safeguard the permanent things, which have converted the brute into the civil social man. In modern politics, the task of *saving* begins with Burke. An intelligent critic honestly may believe Burke to be mistaken; but to deny him the gift of remarkable perception is unjust.

In the citadel of tradition and prescription, Burke keeps vigil. Alive or dead? That depends upon the spirit of the age. For one partisan, the warder of the keep may be Giant Despair; for another, Barbarossa awaiting the trump. Young truth lies just under the wrinkled skin of myth; and a trumpet blast still can tumble our modern Jericho. The tocsin in the Faubourg St. Antoine, in 1789, was such a trump. We may hear another.

Burke the reformer was also Burke the conservator. In

this era of total revolution, thinking men turn almost by instinct to a man of intellect and political practicality who was at once a sagacious improver and an unyielding opponent of revolution.

Ireland, in Burke's day, supported a population greater than it does now; despite the frequent extreme poverty which Burke lamented and endeavored to ameliorate (even in his college days, when he proposed a special tax upon the incomes of absentee landlords), this was not the Ireland of the Potato Famines. Until the middle of Burke's career, revolution was not in the Irish air. Dublin was a true capital, the home of Dean Swift and other famous men whose influence extended far beyond their native land; Trinity College, Dublin's university founded by Queen Elizabeth, maintained stricter standards than did Oxford or Cambridge. Burke and Goldsmith were only two of many men of talent who grew up in Dublin in the first half of the eighteenth century. It was a period of sanguine hopes, rather than of Celtic twilight.

Yet Burke learnt early to love the older rural Ireland. Bookish and sickly as a child, for five years he was sent for his health to live with his mother's kinsmen the Nagles, Roman Catholics, who possessed an estate at Ballyduff, near Castletown Roche, in County Cork, where the romance of old Ireland entered into his soul. Spenser had written the first part of his *Faerie Queene* close by, at Kilcolman Castle, ruined by Burke's time. The whole region was called "the Nagle country." Young Edmund went to school in a crumbling fortalice of the old Nagles, Monanimy Castle, where his teacher, O'Halloran, was one of the ancient breed of "philomaths," hedge school-masters, familiar to modern readers through William Butler Yeats' creation Red Hanrahan, "his little inkpot hanging from his neck by a chain, and his big Virgil and his primer in the skirt of his coat."[4] That devotion to classical and medieval literature which Burke felt all his life commenced here among the ruins. Medieval romances began to haunt the boy like a passion.

Immersed in high and practical concerns of state though he became while still young, it is no wonder that Burke, having grown up in such a land, was loyal lifelong to the immemorial ways, to the life of custom, habit, and faith, the traditions of Goldsmith's "Deserted Village"; seeing Castletown Roche, on the Blackwater, even today, one apprehends at a glance Burke's late denunciation of the "sophisters, calculators, and economists" who, he cried, had extinguished the glory of Europe.

After a brief return to Dublin—where his father's house, now and again flooded by the Liffey, was unhealthy for the boy—Burke was sent to a Quaker school at Ballitore, in County Kildare, kept by a remarkable master, Abraham Shackleton, with whose young son, Richard, Burke formed an enduring friendship. (It is an interesting coincidence that another conservative of genius, Benjamin Disraeli, also was taught by Quakers in his boyhood.) Burke's liking for the members of the Society of Friends also endured, probably influencing his later political activity on behalf of Dissenters.

In his two years at this school, Burke received a good humane discipline, acquiring that admiration for Virgil which runs subtly through his whole view of the social order. It is sufficiently symbolic of the anarchic "antagonist world" against which Burke contended that in 1798, a year after Burke's death, Ballitore became a battleground of the Irish insurrection; the village was plundered and burnt, with atrocities committed by both parties.

One anecdote of the boy's residence at Ballitore, recorded by Richard Shackleton's daughter, suggests that Burke's hatred of arbitrary power, his principle that the same justice shelters duke and cotter, appeared very early:

> A poor man having been compelled to pull down his cabin, because the surveyor of roads declared it stood too near the highway, Burke, who saw the reluctant owner perform his melancholy task, observed with great indignation, that if he were in authority such tyranny should never be exercised with impunity over the defenseless; and he urged his schoolfellows to join in rebuilding the cottage.[5]

At the age of fifteen, in 1744, Burke was enrolled at Trinity College, Dublin. There he obtained a classical scholarship, took part in founding the debating society that still exists, and found time to publish a magazine, the *Reformer*. We know his university years chiefly through his letters to the younger Shackleton.[6] His education was the humanistic discipline described by Sir Thomas Elyot in *The Boke named the Governour,* meant to teach young men to govern themselves and the commonwealth, through close examination of humane letters, in great part; this was reinforced by an early interest in theology. His favorite English authors were Shakespeare, Spenser, Milton, Waller, and Young; among the ancients, he commended Virgil, Cicero, Sallust, Homer, Juvenal, Lucian, Xenophon, and Epictetus. But Burke may be said to have read, as did Samuel Johnson, everything; and, while at Trinity College, he poked into discipline after discipline, confessing to a series of scholarly infatuations—successively, his *furor mathematicus, furor logicus, furor historicus,* and *furor poeticus.*

Sanguine and convivial, the young Burke nevertheless expressed as early as 1746 a foreboding that the complacent, enlightened society of the eighteenth century was not long for this world; that the time was decadent, for all its deceptive flush. Thus he wrote to Shackleton:

> Believe me Dear Dick we are just on the verge of Darkness and one push drives us in—we shall all live, if we live long, to see the prophecy of the Dunciad fulfilled and the age of ignorance come round once more.... [I}s there no one to relieve the world from the curse of obscurity? No not one—I would therefore advise more to your reading the writings of those who have gone before us than our Contemporaries....

And he quoted, in Latin, Virgil's fourth *Eclogue:* "The Saturnian reign returns, and the great order of the centuries is born anew."[7]

Forty-three years later, that came to pass; and in Carlyle's phrase, "On a sudden, the Earth yawns asunder, and amid Tartarean smoke, and glare of fierce brightness, rises Sansculottism, many-headed, fire-breathing, and asks: What think ye of *me?*" Even Burke the undergraduate possessed those curious powers of vaticination which confounded his antagonists after 1789.

At the age of nineteen, while studying at Trinity, Burke wrote the first draft of his *Philosophical Enquiry into the Origins of Our Ideas of the Sublime and Beautiful* (not published until 1757), a highly important contribution to aesthetic theory, which is taken more seriously today than it has been since the end of the eighteenth century.[8] Most young men with literary ambitions turn first to lyric poetry; but Burke, despite his aversion to abstraction and despite his passion for the poets, began with theoretical analysis.

After obtaining the degree of bachelor of arts in 1748, Burke lived on at Trinity College for some months; he may have thought of becoming a don. However this may be, he decided upon the life of a man of letters and public affairs. The character of many professors seems to have repelled him,[9] and a dozen years later he wrote in the *Annual Register:* "He that lives in a college, after his mind is sufficiently stocked with learning, is like a man, who having built and rigged and victualled a ship, should lock her up in a dry dock."[10]

Even before his graduation, the vortex of London was drawing him. In December, 1747, he wrote to Shackleton, referring to their friend William Dennis:

> Don't you think he had money to bear his charges but 'twere his best course to go to London? I am told that a man who writes, can't miss there getting some bread, and possibly good. I heard the other day of a gentleman who maintained himself in the study of the law by writing pamphlets in favour of the ministry.[11]

Although Burke often was at odds with his severe father, the two agreed on one matter: that the young man should take up residence in London. Desiring that his son should become a barrister, the elder Burke sent Edmund to the

Middle Temple in the spring of 1750. From that season forward, London and the home counties of England were the center of Burke's life.

Despite his remarkable literary achievements during his early residence in London, the next nine years remain a period of obscurity in Burke's life. (From 1750 through 1758, only nine of his letters survive.) He found the Inns of Court unsatisfying, for they conveyed merely "narrow and contracted notions," with little reference to jurisprudence.[12] Though he read much law, and the idea of justice dominates his whole thought, gradually he drifted away from the Middle Temple to the profession of letters.

By the middle of the eighteenth century, London already had become what William Cobbett called it with loathing, "The Wen." To it drained the energies of Britain. Despite the obvious superficial differences, in its actual or potential lawlessness, its cosmopolitanism, its riches and poverty cheek by jowl, its consuming of the rural folk who poured by hundreds of thousands into its slums, its coldness and its teeming variety, London was very like the swollen capitals of the twentieth century. "When a man is tired of London, he is tired of life," said Samuel Johnson, "for in London is all that life can afford." Yet it was Johnson himself who had written in 1738 of the great city to which he had made his way from Lichfield:

> Here malice, rapine, accident conspire
> And now a rabble rages, now a fire;
> Their ambush here relentless ruffians lay,
> And here the fell attorney prowls for prey;
> Here falling houses thunder on your head,
> And here a female Atheist talks you dead.

Here Burke, for all his love of rural Ireland, was fixed—like Goldsmith, like Johnson—until his retirement from the House of Commons. The Soho house where he lived later is still standing.

His closest friend during these early London years was a distant kinsman, William Burke, a man of some talent but unlucky in his undertakings, and later not overly scrupulous in his dealings, whom Burke sustained all his life, despite the embarrassments now and again brought upon him by this adventurer. About this time, Burke met a physician from Bath, Dr. Nugent, and his daughter Jane—like Burke, the child of a "mixed marriage." Both Edmund and William Burke wrote sketches of this young lady's character and person.

"She is handsome," Edmund said, "but it is a beauty not arising from features, from complexion and shape. She has all these in a high degree; but whoever looks at her never perceives them, nor makes them the topic of his praise. 'Tis all the sweetness of temper, benevolence, innocence and sensibility which a face can express, that forms her beauty."[13] In March, 1757, Burke married her; and a loving, quiet wife she was. What was rare in fashionable London, after that marriage Burke's name never was associated with that of any other woman.

How did Burke live during these obscure years? By remittances—sometimes grudging—from his father, and perhaps by occasional ghost-writing for Whig politicians (among these, allegedly, Lord Egmont and Lord Granville). But the prospect of marriage required him to seek some livelihood comparatively regular. He turned to his pen; and, had not chance or Providence intervened a few years later, he might have equaled or surpassed Samuel Johnson as a man of letters. In 1756, he published his first book, and for the following three years he was primarily a writer on many themes.

Notwithstanding his strong influence on the course of British and international affairs during his political career, it is as a man of thought and of the pen that Burke lives for us today. Nothing, we are told, is deader than dead politics. Although Burke was a chief architect of the modern political-party system, it is not as a partisan leader that we find him interesting two centuries later. In the end, undoing Goldsmith's criticism of himself, Burke gave to mankind what he owed to party.

From Edmund Burke and Samuel Johnson, more can be learnt than from any other writers of the modern era. This book will be concerned, in part, with party struggles and burning questions of the eighteenth century; yet Burke transcends these. Suspicious though he was, from first to last, of abstract doctrine and theoretic dogma, Burke has obtained his immortality not for what he did, but for what he perceived.

2

From Letters to Politics

A *Vindication of Natural Society,* which brought to Burke his early reputation, was a reply to the dead Bolingbroke; yet it anticipated his more crushing assault upon Rousseau in the last years of Burke's life. Man is not fully man—so ran Burke's lifelong argument—until he is fully civilized; he acquires his higher nature as a member of a culture, of a civil social order. Man's true nature is only latent in the savage.

So *A Vindication* is a most successful exercise in irony. Parodying marvelously Bolingbroke's celebrated style, Burke proceeded to demonstrate that if "natural" religion is preferable to the religious understanding which we have acquired through revelation, right reason, and thousands of years' experience in religious community, then "natural" society must be preferable to the benefits of the just and orderly and free society which we obtain through complex political and economic institutions.

As an example of the ironic phrase, Samuel Johnson once offered this: "Bolingbroke is a holy man." The subtle and free-living Bolingbroke had argued that man does not require the dogmas, doctrines, and institutions of the Christian church, but may repair to a "natural" religion founded upon instinct and private judgment. As the best mode of assailing this fallacy, Burke burlesqued Bolingbroke's theory by suggesting the consequences of such notions when applied to the body politic. Any informed man, he reasoned, can see the absurdity of a "natural" society, suitable only for savages, as a substitute for the intricate social order of Europe, which keeps men from anarchy. By analogy, "natural" religion could only reduce man to anarchy of spirit and morals. For in matters spiritual, as in temporal, we require just authority, the wisdom of our ancestors, and the establishments which have been developed painfully, over many centuries, by men groping for means to know God and to live with themselves and with their fellow men.

Several times in his political career, Burke's opponents unscrupulously endeavored to turn this early book against him, asserting that he had seriously assaulted church and state—though anyone acquainted with Burke knew perfectly well that his ironic masterpiece was the work of a man imbued with Christian learning and tradition, and the most redoubtable defender of political prescription. In the second edition of *A Vindication,* indeed, Burke found it well to declare that he wrote ironically; and on several occasions he repeated this statement, which should have been obvious to any but the illiterate. The attempt of some twentieth-century "philosophical anarchists" to represent Burke as a champion of a "natural," anarchic mode of social existence is sufficiently absurd.

The most interesting quality of this book, writes Sir Herbert Grierson,

is the sidelight that it throws on Burke's temperament, the sensitive, brooding imagination which,
coupled with a restless, speculative intellect, seeking
ever to illuminate facts by principles, gives tone to
Burke's speeches and pamphlets; for it is this temperament which imparts vividness and colour to the
dry details of historical and statistical knowledge, and
it is this temperament which at once directs, keeps in
check, and prescribes its limits to, that speculative,
inquiring intellect. In the sentences in which Burke
paints the lot of those who bear the burden of political
society, the unhappy wretches employed in lead, tin,
iron, copper and coal mines, who scarce ever see the
light of the sun...we get an insight into one of the most
radical characteristics of Burke's mind.... Wise government may lighten the lot of men, it can never make
it more than tolerable for the great majority.[1]

Eleven months later, Burke published *The Sublime and
Beautiful.* Originally written at Trinity College, it was
strongly admired by many critics. Lessing and many other
writers were enduringly influenced by it; and though
Coleridge and most of the other Romantics were impatient
with Burke's theory, nevertheless it wormed its way into
their work. With Sir Joshua Reynolds, Burke became one of
the two chief English theorists of aesthetics in that age—
though he never returned at any length to this subject.

In his emphasis upon the power of the terrible and the
obscure, Burke was breaking with eighteenth-century clas-
sicism. Drawing heavily upon kindred minds of his time,
Burke (in this like David Hume) dissented from the *a priori*
systems of the French *philosophes;* one must observe phe-
nomena and their influence upon mind and heart, rather

than deduce neat conclusions from abstract propositions. The world, Burke saw, was still a place of wonder and obscurity, not a rational construction. "If nothing more," remarks the closest critic of *The Sublime and Beautiful,* "Burke succeeded in stirring the waters of criticism which had tended to stagnate."[2] Burke also penetrates, with considerable originality, into the emotional nature of words, defending their evocative quality, as against the rationalistic argument that words ought to be mere accurate symbols of objective things. In part by a kind of intellectual osmosis, in time his theories came to extend so far as the criticism of Immanuel Kant, the paintings of Henry Fuseli, and the novels of Thomas Hardy.

In his analysis of the sublime and beautiful, as in so much else presently, Burke revolted against what Louis Bredvold calls "the brave new world of the eighteenth century"—that is, the rationalism of the Enlightenment, with its *a priori* assumptions.[3] In part because of his Irishness, he knew that in the arts, as in politics, we neglect the passions only at our peril; in Pascal's phrase, "the Heart has reasons that the Reason cannot know."

As a man of letters, Burke now enjoyed some celebrity— a reputation that later was to become a high and enduring literary fame. In his own day, Johnson said Burke was "the first man everywhere"; Mackintosh, once his adversary, compared him with Shakespeare, and declared that "his works contain an ampler store of political and moral wisdom than can be found in any other writing whatever." Coleridge concluded that "in Burke's writings, indeed, the germs of almost all political truths may be found"; Wordsworth called Burke "by far the greatest man of his age"; William Hazlitt, that astringent critic, though differing from Burke in much, nevertheless remarked, "If there are greater prose writers than Burke, they either lie out of my course of study, or are beyond my sphere of comprehension."

De Quincy was to exclaim, "All hail to Edmund Burke, the supreme writer in his century, the man of largest and finest understanding." Macaulay considered Burke "the greatest man since Milton." Matthew Arnold believed Burke to be the finest master of English prose; Lecky said of his political writings, "The time may come when they will no longer be read. The time will never come in which men would not grow wiser by reading them." There are the words of Leslie Stephen: "Considered simply as a master of English prose, Burke has not, in my judgment, been surpassed in any period of our literature." Lord Acton is most emphatic of all:

> Systems of scientific thought have been built up by famous scholars on fragments that fell from his table. Great literary fortunes have been made by men who traded on the hundredth part of him. Brougham and Lowe lived by the vitality of his ideas. Mackintosh and Macaulay are only Burke trimmed and stripped of all that touched the skies.

Burke's first two books would not by themselves have justified this enthusiasm; yet clearly he was already a man of great talent, and probably of genius. If Burke stands this high with the critics, though he became a politician primarily and a writer only incidentally, what would now be said of him had he spent all his years in the production of history, criticism, humane letters, and philosophy?

Not until Walter Scott's day, however, did the public exist which would make a man affluent solely by the writing of books. Could the young Burke live by his essays and serious journalism, without sinking into Grub Street?

Few men do now, and fewer did then; it had been hard for Samuel Johnson to acquire a competence from letters— and Johnson might not have survived, but for his later pension from the Crown, grateful for his Tory pamphlets. Johnson and Burke met in 1758; Burke already had won the friendship of Dodsley the great bookseller, the Whartons, Dr. Markham, Mrs. Montagu, Bennet Langton, Lord Lyttleton, Mrs. Vesey, Mrs. Elizabeth Carter, Garrick the famous actor, Goldsmith, and other leaders in the London republic of letters. Soon the masterful critic would say of Burke, "I can live very well with Burke; I love his knowledge, his diffusion, and affluence of conversation." Or, on another occasion, Johnson declared, "Yes, Sir, if a man were to go by chance at the same time with Burke under a shed to shun a shower, he would say—'we have had an extraordinary man here.'" (When the Club, Johnson's circle, was formed in 1764, Burke became a member, and proceeded to outshine by his rapid, amusing, and brilliant talk, brogue and all, even Johnson, Garrick, Murphy, Reynolds, and Beauclerk, and the other remarkable men of that society of talkers.)

Most eminently, Burke was what Johnson considered a "clubbable" man. Generous, humorous, passionate, ranging beyond even Johnson in the breadth of his knowledge, he seemed to have looked into everything. His years of outward idleness when he ate his dinners in the Middle

Temple (though disdaining the legal profession), or wandered about the English countryside, had not been wasted. He knew the world, and he knew history, and he knew humane letters, and he knew philosophy, and theology, and the arts (except music, it is said). What was to serve him in greater stead presently, he knew, too: English political institutions. Here was a man who, apparently, might do anything—but for the present, just what? He had a wife to maintain—and, by February, 1758, a son, Richard. Like Johnson, he looked to the booksellers—who, in that day, also were the publishers.

In 1757, he had some hand in a book written chiefly by his comrade Will Burke, *An Account of the European Settlements in America*, foreshadowing his later involvement in American concerns. (In the same year, indeed, he thought seriously of emigrating to America; had his plan not fallen through, the history of two continents might have been interestingly different.) Next year, for Dodsley, he wrote a history of England to the end of the reign of John; part of this was published, but the rest of his intended abridgment of all English history never was set down on paper. "History begins with Burke," Lord Acton was to write, in the Victorian age. Although Burke never found time to complete an historical study on the scale of Hume's or Smollett's, these early works, and the annual historical article which he contributed for three decades to the *Annual Register*, suggest a power of historical vision excelling Macaulay's or Henry Adams'.

This search for meaning in history runs through all Burke's more important speeches and writings. We can surmise the future only through apprehension of the past,

Burke held; and as for the present, Burke anticipated—though not in so many words—Santayana's aphorism that those who ignore the past are condemned to repeat it. History is a record of Providence at work, Burke believed—mysterious though God's ways often are for us. As Burke observed to William Robertson—a more productive but less gifted historian—the failure of public men to read history causes history to consist, in so large a part, of historical judgments upon acts of parliament.

Meanwhile, Burke had contracted with Dodsley to compile and edit a new publication—which continues to this day—*The Annual Register,* concerned with the principal political events and papers, literary and philosophical matters, and startling occurrences of the year, and including various essays and poems. Its first number appeared in June, 1759. For perhaps six years, Burke carried out himself the whole of this formidable task; for a quarter of a century thereafter, he exercised some general supervision and wrote the annual historical article (which remains a principal authority for events in the latter half of the eighteenth century). As Burke said long later, in this exacting work, "I found it necessary to analyze the whole commercial, financial, constitutional, and foreign interests of Great Britain and its empire"—and much else besides. During his first year in Parliament, he nearly collapsed under this literary and editorial burden, and so thereafter entrusted most or much of the volume to others.

Other writers, some of them men of mark, rifled the *Annual Register* from its first appearance: Oliver Goldsmith, as historian, was much indebted to Burke's historical articles; while American historians of the early years of the Republic unhesitatingly plagiarized from the *Register*. Harvey Wish points out that such eminent American historians as David Ramsay, John Marshall, and William Gordon borrowed (in part) not merely Burke's interpretations of colonial affairs, but more frequently his very paragraphs. "Few Englishmen had so profound a knowledge of colonial affairs as did Burke," Wish writes. "His *Annual Register* articles were copious, acutely observant, and warmly sympathetic. Little wonder that the post-revolutionary writers naturally gravitated to them."[4] This is but one of the subtle ways in which Burke's influence eventually spread far beyond England.

The compiling of this annual volume added immensely to Burke's preparation for public life, but it could not pay his way. Unlike the Scots who labored literarily in Samuel Johnson's garret, the Burkes were not frugal. (Both Will Burke, and Edmund's brother Richard, were living in Edmund's household most of this period—as they did, indeed, most of their lives.)[5] Although the *Register* was a remarkable commercial success, for its first several years Burke was paid only a hundred pounds annually; and over the first ten years, he averaged perhaps three hundred pounds per annum, by way of salary. (At his father's death, in 1761, Burke inherited a few thousand pounds; this could not suffice, in London, for the openhanded Burkes.) It became necessary for Edmund to try to combine with the literary profession some other means of obtaining a tolerable livelihood.

Participation in politics might be joined—though somewhat disagreeably—with literary endeavor. In September, 1759, Burke endeavored in vain, through powerful friends, to persuade the elder Pitt to appoint him British consul at Madrid. (Shortly before, William Burke had been made secretary and register of Guadeloupe, taken from the French, and had gone out to his West Indian post; Richard Burke had become a superior kind of supercargo on a West Indian merchant voyage.)

But earlier in that year, Burke had been introduced by Lord Charlemont, the best of Irish peers, to William Gerard Hamilton, then a rising politician of large means and literary interests, generally called "Single-Speech Hamilton" because of his initial (though only) successful address in the House of Commons, four years before. Hamilton required both literary and political assistance; Burke possessed both charm and wisdom; so, by an arrangement somewhat amorphous—it not being clear whether Burke received a salary or only occasional sums of money—Hamilton and Burke agreed to combine forces, as much for the pleasures of serious conversation as for political advancement. Burke was to spend his winters as Hamilton's counselor, his summers working upon his own books. As Johnson did with Lord Chesterfield earlier, so Burke obtained a patron; and as Johnson and Chesterfield parted in acrimony, so eventually did Burke and Hamilton.

In the spring of 1761, Hamilton went over to Dublin as Chief Secretary for Ireland, under the lord lieutenancy of Lord Halifax; and Burke, intimately acquainted with Irish affairs and deep in Irish history, accompanied him as private secretary. They needed to reside in Dublin only during sessions of the Irish Parliament. There Burke began to write a tract against the "Popery Laws" which oppressed Irish Catholics. A perceptive scholar, Walter D. Love, argues convincingly that it was Burke's ardent desire to improve the condition of the Irish, uniting with his financial necessities, which presently persuaded him to relinquish his literary career for the rough-and-tumble of factional politics and parliaments.[6]

Though a great majority in the population, the Irish Catholics had been totally disfranchised ever since the final triumph of the Hanoverians; and though the Penal Laws were no longer enforced ordinarily with full vigor, in theory—and sometimes in practice—the Catholics did not enjoy the equal protection of the laws or even secure tenure of property, and of course could not hold political office. To this cause of discontent was added the poverty of rural Ireland, overpopulated and badly cultivated—the Ireland of Maria Edgeworth's *Castle Rackrent.*

Out of this suffering arose, just before Burke accompanied Hamilton to Dublin, the Whiteboys—night riders in white smocks, violently opposing the enclosure of common lands by the great proprietors, intimidating collectors of tithes, setting fire to stacks and houses—the beginning of Irish rebelliousness that was not to die down until the second decade of the twentieth century, and is not wholly extinguished yet. At least one of Burke's Nagle relatives was accused of participation in this movement. The Whiteboys committed the acts to which nocturnal terrorists usually are given, and Burke did not condone their violence. But he protested vehemently, so far as lay in his power, against the ferocious punishments meted out to captured or alleged Whiteboys. (A proscribed priest and others were put to death cruelly.) An eighteenth-century Titus Oates, an informer of most dubious veracity, arose to testify that the

Whiteboys were privy to a French and Papist plot against the Crown—which charge Burke utterly disbelieved, declaring to his friends that poverty and despair had provoked the disturbances.

Before he crossed to Ireland with Hamilton, Burke wrote concerning these troubles to his friend and lawyer John Ridge, in Dublin:

> For God's sake let me know a little of this matter, and of the history of these new levellers. I see that you have but one way of relieving the poor in Ireland. They call for bread, and you give them 'not a Stone,' but the Gallows.[7]

Though Hamilton, like his secretary, desired Irish reform and was friendly enough to the Catholics, they could not prevail against the Protestant interest in the Irish Parliament. The Chief Secretary had patronage at his disposal, however, and obtained for Burke a pension of three hundred pounds on the Irish establishment—then a usual method of rewarding political services, in lieu of salary.

In 1764, Hamilton fell out with the Duke of Northumberland (who had succeeded Halifax as Lord Lieutenant of Ireland), and was dismissed from his secretaryship. Burke returned to London, never again to exercise direct influence in Ireland—but to contend all his parliamentary years for justice to the Irish generally, and to Irish Catholics particularly.

As Walter Love points out, Burke usually reasoned from circumstance to principle: that is, he saw the things and the men, and then sought for general principles to apply to present discontents. It may be, as Love suggests, that Burke's observations in Ireland helped to lead him to the political philosophy which he expressed with such power after he had left the House of Commons. "Bad government must have provoked thought about what government ought to be, pitching Burke's political thought inevitably upon a level of political theory, rather than letting it remain on the lower level where thought is about concrete dealings with small problems only."[8]

Detesting arbitrary exercise of political power, Burke was led into the four great struggles of his life—his effort to obtain conciliation with the American colonies, his participation in the Rockingham Whigs' contest against the domestic power of George III, his prosecution of Warren Hastings, and his impassioned resistance against Jacobinism, the "armed doctrine." In America, in England, in India, and in France, the denial of justice roused Burke to greatness; for his Dublin Castle years had shown him how order and freedom must be kept in a tolerable balance or tension, that all may be safe together. Irish affairs became the microcosm of his politics.[9]

Back in London, Burke separated himself from Hamilton, much to that politician's discontent. By securing the Irish pension for Burke, Hamilton had hoped that he might obtain indefinitely his secretary-friend's services; when this argument was thrust at him, Burke angrily threw up his pension—though, in law, he might have kept it, even after parting from his patron. Earlier, Hamilton had suggested that Burke might abandon his editorship of the *Annual Register*—with monetary compensation for this sacrifice of income—so that he could spend much more time upon Hamilton's concerns. Burke, however, continued to think of himself as an author, and would not consent to abandon this strong tie to the republic of letters; he felt himself fortunate to have escaped from concerns of state.

As, after leaving the distressed Hamilton, Burke wrote to his friend Charles O'Hara (proprietor of large estates in Sligo), he blessed "Providence every day and every hour to find myself delivered from thoughts and from characters of that kind"—that is (for all his continuing partial involvement in factional politics), from the necessities and compromises of office, despite the attractions of governmental place, with its opportunities for accomplishing something of public benefit.

> But then the walk is certain; there are no contradictions to reconcile; no cross points of honour or interest to adjust; all is clear and open; and the wear and tear of mind, which is saved by keeping aloof from crooked politicks, is a consideration absolutely inestimable.[10]

Samuel Johnson accepted the post of adviser to Hamilton which Burke had vacated. If the great scholar and lexicographer could not live without such connections, how might Edmund Burke? And despite Burke's aversion to "crooked politicks," already he felt something of that call to public duty which had worked upon Cicero, one of Burke's exemplars. Cicero, too, doubtless would have been happier living in retirement at his villas, writing manuals of philosophy; but the times would not permit that to a man of conscience with some experience of public concerns. Thus Burke was drawn again, almost at once, into factional politics—from which he did not depart until the Whigs were torn asunder by the French Revolution.

Almost necessarily, Burke was attracted to one of the Whig factions; for the Tories virtually had ceased to exist, in those days, as a coherent party, and so had nothing to offer a rising man who sought both an opportunity to work for the common good and an opportunity for preferment. His friend Will Burke already was closely associated with Lord Verney, a member of the Whig set led by the Marquis of Rockingham; those were moderate reformers whose principles, vaguely defined though they might be, were akin to the political ideas of Edmund Burke. Should he join the Rockinghams and enter Parliament?

The alternatives were few and unpromising. While associated with Hamilton, Burke had vainly applied for the post of London political agent for the colony of New York; late in 1764, he sought—again to be disappointed—to be made the agent for Grenada and other West Indian islands taken from the French. (Will Burke was back in London, his West Indian appointment terminated by the cession of Guadeloupe back to France.) The Burkes might have attached themselves to some other Whig faction; but the politicians round the Duke of Bedford were a corrupt gang, and the other circles seemed amorphous, unprincipled, or eccentric. Perhaps one might join the Rockingham connection, and yet return later, under circumstances more happy, to the profession of letters.

Ever since their dethroning of James II, in 1688, the Whig magnates had almost monopolized English politics; Bolingbroke's plot to undo them in 1714, at Queen Anne's death, had failed; the Jacobites' resort to arms, in 1705, 1715, and 1745, had been crushed to earth. The first two

Hanoverian kings, interested chiefly in their German territories and unable to speak English coherently, had given little annoyance to Whig dukes, marquises, earls, and other grand politicians. Though the squirearchy remained Tory, for the most part, theirs was a chastened Toryism that, even in 1745, would not save the Pretender from Culloden.

By corruption of Parliament and the electorate, in part, the Whigs had governed. But also they were—many of them—lovers of freedom and private right, disciples of John Locke. They possessed courage, considerable energy (despite their fondness for country-house life), and taste. As Leslie Stephen says, they were invincibly suspicious of parsons—that is, of High Church doctrine and discipline; and often they were allied with the commercial interests. Could anything shake their supremacy? George III, possibly; though he used this or that Whig clique from time to time, he disliked them all mightily. More formidable than the King, perhaps, was the opposition of the chief men of letters and wit about the middle of the eighteenth century: Bolingbroke, Swift, Pope, Johnson. John Locke had been dead a great while. Where might a man of ideas be found who would express their cause with clarity and grace?

It was a time for the moral imagination in politics, if the masters of England were to continue to govern. Discontent already could be detected in America and Ireland; the Tory mob was beginning to growl; demagogues like Wilkes were rising; in India, an empire was being acquired in a fit of absence of mind. George III, employing the Whigs' old tool of corruption, seemed resolved to vindicate Bolingbroke. Samuel Johnson called the Whigs "bottomless." Yet there were among them men of public spirit and strong resolu-

tion who knew that there was more to politics than possession and complacency. Though victorious in the Seven
Years' War, Britain was entering upon new trials and
discontents. Whatever their faults, the Whig nobility and
gentry—unlike the old order of the Continent—were not
decadent, and still knew how to contend against Jacobite
and Jacobin.[11]

The attractive figure of the second Marquis of Rockingham, a gentleman about Burke's own age, was the center
of a group of Whig politicians opposed at once to the
"King's Friends" supporting George III and to the unscru-
pulous Bedford Whigs. At the vast mansion of Wentworth
Woodhouse, in Yorkshire (today a college for training
teachers of physical education), this heir to the great Earl of
Strafford led the leisurely existence shared by so many
English political leaders until the First World War—di-
verted by politics as they were fascinated by the racetrack—
with immense resources to expend upon the inordinately
costly hustings of the eighteenth century. (Even in recent
years, Earl Fitzwilliam, proprietor of Wentworth Woodhouse and remote successor to Burke's Lord Rockingham,
enjoyed an income of a thousand pounds a day.) Will Burke
arranged a meeting between Rockingham and Edmund
Burke; they took to each other. Burke became a member of
the club of Whigs that met frequently at Wildman's tav-
ern—among its members no fewer than four dukes and
nine earls, and such other leading men of politics as Charles
Townshend, Sir William Meredith, Sir William Baker, and
Rockingham himself.

Centering in this club, the Rockingham interest constituted the "legitimate" and often the largest bloc of Whig

strength. William Pitt, soon to be Lord Chatham, also commanded a good deal of Whig support, chiefly among merchants and the bankers of the City; his "genius tinged with madness" was not, however, of the order upon which regular party might be constructed. George Grenville, at this time Prime Minister, commanded his own Whig faction; and there had been, and were yet to be, still other Whig coteries, shifting, merging, quarreling, reorganizing.

Attachment to a particular leader, and desire for office, distinguished these groups one from another more clearly than anything else. But genuine party began to take form among the Whigs who followed the Duke of Cumberland and the Marquis of Rockingham. Bertram Newman describes succinctly the general concepts and aspirations of these Rockingham Whigs:

> They prided themselves on being the real and only depositories of the sacred traditions of 1688; on their aloofness alike from Chatham and his noisy followers in the City of London, and from the corrupt influence of the Bedfords; and they refused to entertain the idea of disturbing the balance of English institutions and incidentally of weakening their own influence by any real measure of parliamentary reform. A main item in their programme, and one which assumed especial prominence when Burke became their philosopher, was to keep the Crown in its place by means of an organized party and cabinet system in the modern sense.[12]

During the year which followed his return from Ireland, Burke acquired considerable reputation among the Rockinghams. He was a man of thought, they perceived;

and they had need of such. He might give order and
coherence to their ideas. Moreover, Burke fascinated: he
was a good companion; no one equaled him in talk; his
mind was astoundingly quick; he could dispatch business
better than any of them; and he might be trusted.

Hope sustained the Rockinghams, who expected that
soon they would take office, and hold it for a long while.
Triumphant over France two years before, England might
now go about internal improvement and colonial expansion; and the Rockinghams would supply leadership. Their
first expectation was gratified, but the second disappointed;
and by joining them, as matters turned out, Burke condemned himself—badly though he needed the salary of
office—to a parliamentary career spent almost wholly in
opposition. Despite tempting offers on occasion from other
factions, he was to remain throughout loyal to the political
friends he had acquired in 1765.

Somewhat abruptly, the Grenville ministry was dismissed
in July, 1765; the Grenvilles, Bedfords, King's Friends, and
Tories who had composed the government vacated their
places. Not the erratic and haughty Pitt, but Lord Rockingham, was invited to form the new government—on the
recommendation of the Duke of Cumberland to the reluctant King. Accepting power, Rockingham asked Burke to
become his private secretary; and then, as now, sometimes
the private secretary to the first lord of the treasury was a
man of mark. Thus for the first time Edmund Burke found
himself at the center of power; and Will Burke took office,
too, as an Undersecretary of State.

Edmund Burke was not merely Rockingham's right hand,
but both his hands, as Lord Buckinghamshire wrote to

Grenville—"a metaphysician, a man of learning and imagination," descending from a garret (or so Buckinghamshire put it) to the head of administration. Burke himself wrote to Charles O'Hara:

> I have got an employment of a kind humble enough; but which may be worked into some sort of consideration, or at least advantage; Private Secretary to Lord Rockingham, who has the reputation of a man of honour and integrity; and with whom, as they say, it is not difficult to live.[13]

The private secretaryship, nevertheless—this is typical enough of most of Burke's years in politics—paid no salary, and Rockingham did not find for Burke the sinecure usually attached to the post. (From his long connection with Rockingham, indeed, Burke obtained large loans, forgiven at Rockingham's death, and less frequent gifts of no great sum; but it was a service uncertain and not very lucrative.) Certainly two hundred and fifty pounds, and possibly somewhat more, was paid to Burke by Rockingham's authorization from the Secret Service Fund—then the usual way of furnishing some compensation to unsalaried members of the ministry; yet this was a pittance for Burke's tremendous labors on behalf of the Rockingham government; he was, in effect, a manager of the party and parliamentary chief whip, as well as the government's man of ideas.

Such a one must have a seat in the House of Commons. Lord Verney, the rich Irish peer to whom Will Burke was close, had in his pocket the borough of Wendover; William Burke declined this seat, in Edmund's favor; and on December 23, 1765, the electors of Wendover chose the talented Irishman to represent them. "Yesterday I was elected for Wendover," Burke wrote to O'Hara, "got drunk, and this day have a heavy cold."[14]

That evening's exhilaration at Wendover, with its toasts to Burke and to John Wilkes (which demagogue, really, Burke despised), and to liberty, was succeeded by misgivings. Two years later, Burke wrote to O'Hara of his first days as a member of Parliament:

> Every body congratulated me on coming into the House of Commons, as being in the certain Road of a great and speedy fortune; and when I began to be heard with some little attention, every one of my friends was sanguine. But in truth I never was so myself. I came into Parliament not at all as a place of preferment, but of refuge; I was pushed into it; and I must have been a Member, and that too with some Eclat, or be a little worse than nothing; such were the attempts made to ruin me when I first began to meddle in Business. But I considered my situation on the side of fortune as very precarious. I looked on myself, with this New Duty upon me, as a man devoted; and thinking in this manner, nothing has happened that I did not expect, and was not well prepared for.[15]

Burke's first parliamentary speeches were wonderfully successful—which mattered much, in those times. Samuel Johnson commented, "He made two speeches in the House for repealing the Stamp Act, which were publicly commended by Mr. Pitt, and have filled the town with wonder. Burke is a great man by nature, and is expected soon to achieve civil greatness." And this praise came from the man who had declared that the first Whig was the Devil.

Yet Burke's "refuge" in place—though not in St. Stephen's Chapel—was to be of brief duration; it was as well that he entertained no lofty expectations of fortune from it. Even then, it is clear, he thought of practical politics as no better than an unhappy alternative to a life spent upon philosophy and literature. Not until he had become hotly entangled in the struggles over American and Indian affairs, and in domestic reform, did he find, with Cicero, that the career of the statesman may provide occasions and themes for the moral imagination and the literary genius.

Grenville had passed the Stamp Act before leaving office: thus the Rockinghams were plunged at once into the current of events which would lead, within a decade, to the fights at Lexington and Concord, and to the Declaration of Independence. In the compass of this little book about Burke, one can examine with any closeness only the principal causes and issues which Burke encountered during his public life; otherwise one wanders bewildered in the petrified forest of withered controversies; and as John Henry Newman put it, if we wish to know anything, we must resign ourselves to being ignorant of much. The chief occupation of Burke's first decade in Parliament was the crisis of the North American colonies. In their endeavor at conciliation, Burke and his party failed; yet out of the debate arose much of Burke's political wisdom. The following chapter, accordingly, deals with Burke on America, to the partial exclusion of lesser concerns which were Burke's between 1766 and 1777.

The philosopher in action: that was Burke's description

of the accomplished statesman. He was now thirty-six years old, and prepared for political action, upon a philosophical foundation, if ever man might be. For the next twenty-nine years, he would fight in the thick of the political press, caught up in every quarrel of the hour; and then, retiring from Parliament, he would hold his pen again—to exert at the last a practical power given to very few authors and men of intellect.

3

Conciliation and Prudence

In the last third of the eighteenth century, Britain was losing an empire in North America and enlarging another in India. Edmund Burke, though he never visited either America or India, had a consuming interest in both, throughout his three decades in Parliament. Ireland, too, was an imperial problem, and he expended no little of his energies upon the affairs of his native land. Simultaneously, he was contending against the ambition of the King at home, holding together a party, advocating governmental reforms, and constructing a body of principles meant to preserve the British constitution and to adapt that constitution to the new age. (The true statesman, he said, joins to a disposition to preserve an ability to reform.) Finally, he was compelled to turn philosopher, that Christian and European civilization might withstand armed doctrine.

For the sake of clarity, these principal fields of activity are treated separately (for the most part) in the following chapters, even though chronologically they overlapped or coincided in some degree. Roughly speaking, however, the sequence of these concerns was as follows: first, the American Revolution; second, the struggle with the King, including the Economical Reform; third, the affairs of India; finally, the French Revolution. The Irish question runs parallel with all these struggles, growing more grave as the years pass.

The first enormous question which Burke confronted— indeed, on the very day that he took his seat in the House of Commons—was the hurricane brewing in the North American colonies. That labor—though, in terms of practical success, it was the least enduring of Burke's undertakings—remained until very recently the aspect of Burke best known to Americans.

An erroneous popular impression long persisted in America that somehow Burke was "in favor" of the American revolutionary cause. In truth, Burke never smiled upon any revolution—with the exception of the "Glorious Revolution" of 1688, which, he said, was a revolution not made, but prevented, and therefore no revolution at all. He did, true enough, sympathize with some of the complaints of the more moderate American opponents of George III's rigorous colonial policies. But revolution, and separation from the Empire, he believed to be great evils; by timely concession and compromise, these might yet be averted, the Rockingham Whigs hoped.

Here we cannot review at any length the causes and course of the American movement toward independence. Perhaps the breach could not have been averted by any means. After the peace of 1763, the American colonies no longer required British protection against the French.

Rapidly increasing in numbers and prosperity, and separated by the Atlantic from King and Parliament, more than two million Americans of European descent naturally inclined toward self-government. Then, too, the old mercantilistic system, expressed in the Navigation Acts, was giving at the seams; soon its theoretical base would be undermined by Adam Smith; it could not coincide much longer with the economic interest of the Thirteen Colonies. Yet the rupture might have been postponed, or some loose connection with the British Empire retained almost indefinitely, had not George III and the majority in Parliament insisted upon asserting claims of absolute suzerainty which they could not enforce.

The immediate dispute was as to whether, and how, the North American colonies should pay a share of the military defense of the Empire. During the Seven Years' War, the several colonial assemblies had voted voluntary grants in aid of operations against the French; but sometimes these appropriations had been tardy, and sometimes niggardly. An attempt to raise revenue for this purpose on a regular basis, by either "external" or "internal" taxation of the colonies, was the fundamental error of the King and most of his ministers. Though this royal claim was neither unreasonable nor unjust, it was unseasonable, the French menace being terminated; and it fell into conflict with the swelling pride of the colonists, who claimed all the "rights of Englishmen"—or, in fact, somewhat more than the rights possessed by the King's subjects in Great Britain and Ireland.

The assertions of the American patriots—and, on occasion, of Burke—notwithstanding, George III was neither a tyrant nor a fool. Rather, he was a very stubborn king of limited talents. He meant himself to be a patriot: Bolingbroke's Tory manual, *The Patriot King,* was in the forefront of his mind. Often he looked upon himself as the champion of the common good, or of the English people, against the Whig oligarchy which, in his eyes as in Bolingbroke's, had usurped prescriptive royal authority. When at last he died (years after Burke), though he had been mad for years, he was immensely mourned by the people. (In contrast, the French had stood in sullen silence as Louis XIV was borne to his tomb, had hooted the funeral procession of Louis XV, and had not waited for the natural death of that well-meaning monarch Louis XVI.) Though he forfeited an empire by his imprudence, George was a sovereign of good private character and good heart, the first real Englishman of the House of Hanover, but obsessed by notions of absolute royal prerogative, and—not scrupulous in his means—contending obdurately against the whole political drift of the age, at home and overseas.

Burke fought the King and most of his ministers for thirty years; he opposed George with particular bitterness during the struggle over American policy, believing that should the King succeed in diminishing American liberties, at once he would turn to English policies as arbitrary as those of James II. Yet to the institution of the Crown he was loyal always; and when radicals commenced to talk of "cashiering kings," in the French fashion, Burke (changing his front but not his ground) turned upon such foes of the old constitution with a vigor exceeding even that he had put forth against the aspirations of George III.

"Their reverence for church and crown, for history and tradition, their preference for the organic society instead of the atomistic natural rights philosophy of the eighteenth-century revolutionaries, made them enemies of the Foxite Whigs," writes Carl Cone, of Burke and his friends.

> If Burke and the Rockingham Whigs fought George's efforts to play the Patriot King for the first thirty years of his reign, those of their followers who later became Tories supported the crown for the last thirty years, when George was no longer capable of the party leadership he had displayed in his youth.[1]

In 1766, however, this turn could not be foreseen. With Lord Rockingham, Burke had entered the King's ministry—though only because George had come to detest Grenville even more than he did Rockingham; he was the closet philosopher of the first lord of the treasury; and he, with the prime minister, had to seek for means to conciliate the angered British subjects of North America. They must walk carefully; they knew they were not beloved by George (who sometimes acted as if Rockingham did not exist); while the more irascible among the colonists were at least as stubborn as the King. What compromise might be contrived, reconciling liberty and order?

Already, from Boston to Savannah, the slogan "no taxation without representation" was being uttered. The colonial leaders were not wholly candid. They disliked any direct taxation; if they might help it, they would not be taxed at all. But as for representation in Parliament, they had no real desire for that, either. Even had they been represented in proportion to their numbers, still they would have been hopelessly outvoted at Westminster, in any contest of interest; at best, they could have constituted—so represented—no more than an irritant to English power, as did the Irish members after the Irish Act of Union. Besides, some token colonial representation in Parliament would not have recognized fully the population or aspirations of America—not in the unreformed Parliament of the eighteenth century; the House of Commons then gave more weight to the rotten and pocket boroughs of Cornwall than to the whole of Scotland. Finally, Boston and New York and Philadelphia were too distant from London for effective participation in the Mother of Parliaments. The colonial "Patriot" politicians really desired neither taxation nor representation; they sought effective autonomy.[2]

Grenville's Stamp Act, desperately unpopular as direct taxation and as the intended means for supporting a permanent civil and military establishment of the Crown in North America, had provoked the colonists to think of insurrection. Thus the first necessity of the Rockingham government was to remove the cause of discontent, while still asserting royal and parliamentary supremacy over North America, and satisfying the King that they were not feebly yielding to colonial insolence. (Some important members of Rockingham's ministry had been chosen at George's insistence, and they, too, must be conciliated.) In their determination to repeal the odious Stamp Act, the Rockinghams had the powerful support of William Pitt and his faction—who, going further than Rockingham, Burke, and the cabinet, declared that any form of taxation of the colonies was unconstitutional.

Promptly the speeches of Pitt and Burke prevailed: the Stamp Act was repealed. But Parliament and Privy Council, in part to placate the King, also passed the Declaratory Act, asserting the right of the Crown in Parliament to legislate for the colonies (though omitting any direct reference to taxation). This satisfied reasonably well, for different reasons, both the King and Pitt; yet it was to remain a thorn in the flesh of the more radical colonial leaders, who maintained that though they owed allegiance to the Crown, they were not constitutionally subject to Parliament, since unrepresented at Westminster.

Whether or not the Declaratory Act was prudent, it was a sincere expression of Burke's convictions. Somewhere sovereignty must reside; the British Empire was governed by the Crown in Parliament, not by royal authority alone; the colonies could not be at once beneficiaries of the imperial system, entitled to the protection of the Crown, and yet theoretically altogether independent of Parliament. In practice, Burke would have exempted the colonies from taxation, having Britain be satisfied, instead, with the commercial benefits of trade with North America; but in logic and constitutional theory, he acknowledged the right of the Crown to govern North America—and, if need be, to tax, quite as English and Scots and Irish were taxed.

Nor did he desire that Americans obtain seats in the House of Commons. That project was impractical. Besides, as he had written in the *Annual Register* for 1765, to give constituencies to colonies that admitted the institution of slavery would be inconsonant with the character of Parliament: "...common sense, nay self-preservation, seems to forbid, that those who allow themselves unlimited right over the liberties and lives of others, should have any share in making laws for those who have long renounced such unjust and cruel distinctions."[3] He might have added that, liking scarcely better the Puritanism of New England, he would have been dismayed to see the "dissidence of dissent," as a bloc, speechifying in St. Stephen's Hall.[4]

The repeal of the Stamp Act and the adoption of the Declaratory Act were almost the only important accomplishments of the first Rockingham ministry, which endured for but a few months. Pitt, with his popular appeal, seemed more useful to the King than did Rockingham; and also, despite his opinion that any taxation of the colonies was unconstitutional, Pitt was more resolved than Rockingham that the colonial assemblies must be compelled to acknowledge royal and parliamentary authority. Rockingham, Burke, and their colleagues did succeed, nevertheless, in modifying Grenville's Revenue Act. Their bill removed the preferential duties on molasses imported to North America—particularly by New England—from the West Indies, which trade the Grenville measure of 1764 had made a virtual monopoly of the British West India planters. Against the opposition of Pitt, free ports were designated in the West Indies, so that the rum-distillers of New England might buy molasses from Spanish and French sources on tolerable terms; British and foreign molasses were to be taxed at the same rate. Certain other duties obnoxious to the colonial assemblies were diminished or abandoned. Together with the repeal of the Stamp Act, these measures made Burke one of the English politicians most popular in America.

Rockingham's policies, all the same, had not been conspicuously popular in Parliament or with the English people, except for such mercantile constituencies as Bristol. The Rockinghams had served the King's turn; now Rockingham might be dismissed with impunity, giving way to the "Great Commoner," Pitt—who, in July, 1766, was elevated to a peerage. Lord Rockingham departed from office; and his whole reforming faction went into the political wilderness, to enjoy power again for only one brief interval, years later.

Pitt and the Duke of Grafton (who succeeded Rockingham at the Treasury) had no place for Burke. Though Rockingham authorized Burke, Dowdeswell, and his other followers to take office under the new government, the clever Irishman was not liked by the new ministry, nor had he much relish for them. He made a visit to Ireland; when he returned, the Rockinghams were in thorough opposition to Pitt and Grafton, and to the end of the American Revolution the Whigs remained divided over American policy. Burke had become already what he was to remain—except for two short intervals—to the end of his parliamentary years, a leader of the opposition.

It was a period of much travail for Burke, this time when the Revolution approached; when, presently, the Rockinghams conducted an ineffectual opposition to the conduct of the war itself, making them unpopular; when his deep involvement in Indian affairs commenced; when Ireland glowered; when he was required to defend his actions before the electors of Bristol; when he gave principle to the Rockingham Whigs, founding the first—if rudimentary—modern political party. Moreover, he was in financial distress during most of this time. Yet this was the era in which he produced three works (two of them speeches soon published as pamphlets) which John Morley called his finest: the *Speech on American Taxation,* the *Speech on Moving Resolutions for Conciliation with the Colonies,* and the *Letter to the Sheriffs of Bristol.* In Morley's words, "It is no exaggeration to say that they compose the most perfect manual in our literature, or any literature, for one who approaches the study of public affairs, whether for knowledge or for practice."[5]

At the commencement of this long period of opposition, Burke's prospects seemed fair enough. About the time the Rockinghams began to slip from power, Lord Verney and William Burke had embarked upon heavy speculation in the stock of the East India Company. (Edmund later declared, truthfully, that he never held East India stock.) In part through political pressure, the proprietors of the Company were compelled to increase their dividend from six to ten per cent. Will Burke (who kept virtually a common purse with Edmund, lived with him, and apparently expected to help pay for their country residence) had the beginning—on paper—of a tolerable fortune. So heartened, in the spring of 1768 Edmund Burke purchased the beautiful estate of Gregories, near Beaconsfield: a charming grand house a century old, a farm, and six hundred acres—with, besides, an admirable library and a much praised collection of paintings and sculpture. The price was high, but so were Burke's expectations. A stake in the country was considered essential for any member of Parliament then; and had Burke ever stood for election as a county member, he would have had to possess, to qualify, a property yielding an income of three hundred pounds a year.

This purchase was a grave miscalculation. In May, 1769, the East India shares fell catastrophically (though only temporarily). The Burkes were nearly ruined; Lord Verney was hard hit; Gregories was almost lost. Thereafter, all his days, Burke was burdened with gigantic debts, which his widow did not succeed in paying entirely until some years after Burke was buried at Beaconsfield, despite Burke's pension and the eventual sale of Gregories by Mrs. Burke. Worse, Will's political manipulations to increase or hold constant the price of East India stock had involved Edmund, damaging his reputation.[6]

An incidental consequence of this affair, four years later, was Burke's loss of the parliamentary seat at Wendover: Lord Verney, requiring money, felt it necessary to sell his interest in the constituency to the highest bidder (a common practice in the days of rotten and pocket boroughs), and Burke was in no condition to bid. To save his friend's place in the House of Commons, Lord Rockingham contrived that Burke should be chosen by the electors of Malton, a borough substantially in Rockingham's gift. Yet no sooner had this occurred than Burke was invited to stand for election as one of the two members of Parliament for the commercial constituency of Bristol, then the second city of England, where the Rockingham reforms of the tariffs and other Rockingham measures were popular. Resigning from Malton, in October, 1774, Burke became a member for Bristol. In his address to the electors of that port, he informed them that he would vote in Parliament as he thought wisest, not necessarily according to their wishes of the moment, where particular measures were in question. Six years later, he learned that Bristol would not abide such independence in a representative.[7]

While these events in Burke's life occurred, the Rockingham Whigs contended against Lord Chatham's administration, which adopted Townshend's Revenue Act, enraging the colonists afresh; at the same time Pitt (now Lord Chatham), Grafton, and their colleagues had enacted the New York Restraining Act, punishing New York for disobedience to Parliament by forbidding the governor of New York to approve any legislation of the New York Assembly until New York should comply with the Mutiny Act. Townshend's duties on glass, paper, lead for paint, and tea were meant to finance a royal colonial administration independent of appropriations from the colonial assemblies. Thus Rockingham's and Burke's brief work of conciliation was undone, and the Boston Tea Party cast its shadow before.

We cannot recount here the weary story of the approach of the Revolution, through changes of ministry and policy, tempers steadily rising higher on either side of the Atlantic. The King, the King's Friends, and the Bedford Whigs must bear much of the blame. For nearly three years the Rockinghams remained disheartened and comparatively quiet; but at the beginning of 1769, Burke spoke repeatedly against measures of increasing severity and dubious legality on the part of the government, particularly the Duke of Bedford's motion (adopted on February 8, 1769) to transport to trial in England subjects accused of treason. His arguments against Townshend's duties, though delivered somewhat tardily, began to have weight in the Commons.

Burke's American popularity soon stood at its height. A friend of the colonists he was, of course; but no friend of revolution: thus he said, in 1770, concerning parliamentary reform at home, "Indeed, all that wise men ever aim at is to keep things from coming to the worst. Those who expect perfect reformations, either deceive or are deceived miserably." In the colonies, many of those whose views stood closest to his own presently were denounced as "Tories." (In reality, the genuine Tory was a rare bird in America; much of the so-called "Tory" faction during the Revolution—equal in numbers, according to John Adams, to the Patriots—was composed of colonials who held Rockingham Whig convictions.)

Still, in the minds of many American zealots for "no taxation without representation," Burke was a radical champion, the ally of John Wilkes. Privately, the Rockinghams detested and dreaded Wilkes, as mob-leader, blasphemer, and rogue; publicly, they assumed a pose of neutrality, or sometimes of sympathy; Burke had some part in the parliamentary defense of Wilkes, and in private negotiations to persuade him to return to his French exile, lest he embarrass the Rockinghams further. The aristocratic Rockingham Whigs wanted no demagogues or fanatics with mobs at their back to intimidate Parliament, officers of the Crown, and magistrates; and the rousing of the rabble by Wilkes was a foretaste of what would come to London, in 1780, with the Gordon Riots.

The Grafton administration fell in January, 1770 (Chatham having dropped out previously), and there came to head the government Lord North, wholly obedient to the King. The Rockinghams, joined by Grenville and his followers, concentrated their opposition upon the ruinous American policy. Burke's attacks upon Lord North, if sometimes intemperate, confirmed the Americans in their high opinion of the member from Wendover; while North has remained ever since something of a bogeyman to most American historians. Really, Lord North was a tolerant, good-natured, competent politician, with nothing of the despot in him, privately often on cordial terms with Burke, whose talents he admired.[8] (Burke came to demand North's impeachment, and Fox to demand North's head; the Prime Minister dozed placidly during their fulminations.) On March 5, the Boston "Massacre" happened. Surely the denouncer of North must be attached to the American cause! Such considerations presumably had a part in the choosing by the New York Assembly of Burke as their London agent, in 1771—a post he had sought, lucklessly, a decade earlier.

Today such an appointment would be criticized—to put matters mildly—as involving a conflict of interests; but it was then usual for members of the House of Commons to become, with everybody's knowledge, paid agents—lobbyists, almost—for colonies or other groups with serious concerns at Court or Parliament. This post, for which Burke was rewarded by a welcome five hundred pounds a year, did not require him to alter his previous views, or even to be more active in opposition to the North ministry; it did, however, serve to inform him more fully about American affairs.

O'Hara congratulated him: "It is a mark of the approbation of a people, and therefore more welcome than any favour from a single man. It leaves you free to your own pursuits, both in politics and in farming."[9] At first, the agency cost Burke little in energy, and did not even involve him in hotter disputes with the government. As Ross Hoffman finds, "Burke's duties as agent certainly were not large and could not have occupied more than a minute fraction of his time. No serious difficulties arose between the province and the imperial government at London; nor did any American questions come before Parliament from 1771 to 1774 to pose the issue of the compatibility of his activities as colonial agent with his duties as member of Parliament."[10] New York was not turbulent Massachusetts (for which colony Dr. Benjamin Franklin was then London agent). During much of this period, Burke was preoccupied with East Indian affairs.

But on December 16, 1773, pseudo-Indians threw overboard, in Boston harbor, a whole shipload of tea. Shortly after taking office, North had repealed most of the Townshend duties, but had retained the heavy tax on tea. Men of the kidney of Samuel Adams would not pay it, nor permit it to be paid.

North retaliated with the Boston Port Act, passed by a heavy majority in both houses of Parliament; Boston was to be strangled economically. Only Burke and William Dowdeswell protested vehemently. "One town in proscription, the rest in rebellion, can never be a remedial measure for general disturbances," Burke told the ministers. "Have you considered whether you have troops and ships sufficient to enforce an universal proscription to the trade of the whole continent of Europe? If you have not, the attempt is childish, and the operation fruitless."

On April 19, 1774, Burke delivered a general assault upon the North policy—his celebrated speech on American Taxation. Some of his previous activity in American affairs had been inconsistent, tempered to suit such occasional allies as Grenville, or partially unjust to the ministry. Now, however, he did become the philosopher in action, appealing for prudence, as opposed to abstract assertions of imprescriptible right; he made clear his enduring principle that for the statesman, prudence is the primary virtue.

The duty on tea, said Burke, must be repealed for the sake of tolerable relations with America, for the sake of the East India Company (caught hopelessly between Scylla and Charybdis, in Boston harbor), and, most of all, for the sake of the British imperial system, with all its benefits. America should not be taxed to raise British revenue, for the Navigation Laws provided sufficient advantage to Britain, through the promotion of trade; as bad, British India might be ruined through the stifling of the market for tea. Taxation of colonies should be resorted to only in emergency, if a colony had refused to contribute money for the common defense; the "inferior legislatures" within the British Empire ordinarily should manage the concerns of the people whom they represented, even though by right, as expressed in the Declaratory Act, the British Parliament—or, more properly speaking, the King in Parliament, a kind of legislative trinity—reserved the sovereign power to govern the whole empire.

The essence of Burke's brief is in this paragraph:

> Again, and again, revert to your old principles—seek peace and ensure it—leave America, if she has taxable matter in her, to tax herself. I am not here going into the distinctions of rights, nor attempting to mark their boundaries; I hate the very sound of them.

Leave the Americans as they anciently stood, and these distinctions, born of our unhappy contest, will die along with it. They and we, and their and our ancestors, have been happy under that system. Let the memory of all actions in contradiction of that good old mode, on both sides, be extinguished forever. Be content to bind America by laws of trade; you have always done it. Let this be your reason for binding their trade. Do not burden them by taxes; you were not used to do so from the beginning. Let this be your reason for not taxing. These are the arguments of states and kingdoms. Leave the rest to the schools; for there only may they be discussed with safety. But if, intemperately, unwisely, fatally, you sophisticate and poison the very source of government, by urging subtle deductions, and consequences odious to those you govern, from the unlimited and illimitable nature of supreme sovereignty, you will teach them by these means to call that sovereignty itself in question. When you drive him hard, the boar will surely turn upon the hunters. If that sovereignty and their freedom cannot be reconciled, which will they take? They will cast your sovereignty in your face. Nobody will be argued into slavery.

Custom and usage, in fine, are firm ground for justice and for voluntary acceptance of necessary authority; pushing claims of abstract right upon metaphysical premises, and endeavoring to govern the commonwealth by notions of perfection, must end in setting interest against interest. Accustomed to a high degree of liberty, the Americans must be indulged in their old ways; and the whole empire would prosper by this prudent avoidance of extreme doctrines.

Powerful though this address was, it altered few votes. Sir Joshua Reynolds once inquired why Burke took such trouble with a speech, "knowing that not one vote would be gained by it." Burke replied that a member of Parliament gains reputation and influence by good speeches; and that, even though the majority's decision may go against the orator's views, still strong and eloquent arguments may modify a bill, by impressing the majority with the strength of opposing views. Then, too, he concluded,

> The House of Commons is a mixed body; I except the minority, which I hold to be pure [*smiling*], but I take the whole House. It is a mass by no means pure, but neither is it wholly corrupt, though there is a large proportion of corruption in it. There are many members who generally go with the Minister who will not go all lengths. There are many honest well-meaning country gentlemen who are in Parliament only to keep up the consequence of their families. Upon most of these a good speech will have influence.

But this was not such an occasion. Early in May, Parliament approved two severe bills, making the Massachusetts constitution far more amenable to royal authority, and altering that colony's courts. The stern spirit of the Bay Colony would not submit to this.

New York, too, was preparing to resist the duty on tea. Almost as Burke spoke on American Taxation, action commenced. The acting governor of New York was eighty-seven years old, and unable to resist effectively the "Mohawks" who, going aboard the vessel "London," held New York's Tea Party. To prevent radicals from seizing control of the protest against the Boston Port Act, the conservative proprietors and merchants who were Burke's New York principals and correspondents—the Delanceys, Crugers, and others—now joined a committee to defend the rights of all the colonies. Burke's still was a great name with the American radicals, and to them these sober New York gentlemen quoted his counsels of prudence, discouraging rash action.

But the ministry would not return to the old policy of salutary neglect. On June 13, the House of Commons passed the Quebec Act, intended in part to use Canada as a counterpoise against the English-speaking colonies. Burke's protests on behalf of the Rockinghams and of New York were unavailing, of course, as had been his earlier appeals for conciliatory measures. New York and Pennsylvania, previously less restive than New England and Virginia, now were thoroughly alarmed. The first Continental Congress was taking form; the Patriot delegates met at Philadelphia in September, to concert colonial resistance short of rebellion, if possible. It was the beginning of the end of British authority in the Thirteen Colonies.

By early February, 1775, Lord North was pushing for a declaration that Massachusetts was in rebellion; Parliament so resolved. Later in the month, further steps were authorized for subduing resistance in America. In March, North extended the restraints to four more colonies.

Late in February, North had induced Parliament to offer certain conciliatory proposals to the Americans, chiefly a scheme to abandon taxation (though not the *right* to tax) if the colonial assemblies would promise to make grants at the Crown's request—the amount of every grant, and its use, to be determined by the English government. This plan was impractical, Burke thought; and the colonists would not put their trust in the word of North. On March 22, therefore, Burke delivered his most famous speech, "On Moving Resolutions for Conciliation with America": this was the opposition's alternative.

The grand plea was twice vain: there was no possibility that Parliament would be won over by Burke and the Rockinghams, at this hour; and by April 19, Paul Revere had ridden, the shots heard round the world were fired at Lexington, and Bunker Hill was in prospect. The Revolution had commenced a month before "Conciliation" was published as a pamphlet, and well before word of Burke's speech had reached America.

But as a piece of political wisdom, the Speech on Conciliation has endured down to our time, and does not ring hollow today. Both Lord Chatham and Horace Walpole, no friends of Burke, praised this address heartily. The House of Commons voted down his first resolution by 270 to 78; yet posterity voted with Burke.

"A great empire and little minds go ill together." Burke's six conciliatory resolutions amounted to a formal admission that the colonies lacked representation in Parliament; that taxation without representation had produced severe discontent; that the distance of the colonies from England, and other circumstances, had made representation in Parliament impractical; that colonial assemblies were competent to levy taxes; that the assemblies had made voluntary grants to the Crown for the common defense; that such voluntary grants from the colonial assemblies were more agreeable to colonial subjects, and accorded better with the imperial interest, than taxation by Parliament. His appeal was to English generosity and imperial prosperity. The speech added little to Burke's previous arguments on this subject, but so combined rational exposition, moral imagination, and passionate intensity that it has been ever since the principal school-model of English eloquence.

Perhaps, as Carl Cone comments, Burke's proposals would not have satisfied the American patriots, even had Parliament embraced them and even had there been opportunity for discussion in the colonies. They did not touch upon the Navigation Acts, which in general Burke had defended; and the mercantilism of that system for regulating commerce was bound up with American discontents, even though the colonial declarations of grievances did not emphasize this point. Yet had Burke and the Rockinghams not gone out of office years before, Burke's program, adopted earlier, might possibly have been a basis for compromise and gradual accommodation and reform.

Burke declared that he did not know the method of drawing up an indictment against a whole people. The ministry's measures were directed not merely against the extreme "Patriots," but were calculated to ruin all North Americans.

> The mode of inquisition and dragooning is going out of fashion in the Old World, and I should not confide much to their efficacy in the New. The education of the Americans is also on the same unalterable bottom of their religion. You cannot persuade them to burn their books of curious science, to banish their lawyers from their courts of law, or to quench the lights of their assemblies by refusing to choose those persons who are best read in their privileges. It would

> be no less impracticable to think of wholly annihilat-
> ing the popular assemblies in which these lawyers sit.
> The army, by which we must govern in their place,
> would be far more chargeable to us, not quite so
> effectual, and perhaps, in the end, full as difficult to
> be kept in obedience.

In denying the Americans their prescriptive liberties, Burke continued, the Crown must imperil the chartered rights of Englishmen. "As we must give away some natural liberties to enjoy civil advantages, so we must sacrifice some civil liberties for the advantages to be derived from the communion and fellowship of a great empire." But any Englishman would rather risk his life than submit to an arbitrary government.

> In every arduous enterprise we consider what we are
> to lose as well as what we are to gain; and the more and
> better stake of liberty every people possess, the less
> they will hazard in an attempt to make it more. These
> are *the cords of man.* Man acts from adequate motives
> relative to his interest, and not on metaphysical
> speculations. Aristotle, the great master of reason-
> ing, cautions us, and with great weight and propri-
> ety, against this species of delusive geometrical accu-
> racy in moral arguments, the most fallacious of all
> sophistry.

Britain, abandoning insistence upon the full exercise of abstract sovereignty, should settle in this time for the possible. Such was the gist of these three hours of noble rhetoric.

Though the war had commenced, might it not be

arrested, even now? Burke still hoped that something might be done by an energetic appeal to the English people, who could petition Parliament for peace; but he found Lord Rockingham and his whole following discouraged and fainthearted. Desperate, he urged Rockingham to employ his powerful influence in Ireland to persuade the Irish Parliament to refuse to contribute troops and supplies to the American campaign; Ireland might mediate the quarrel. Of this, too, nothing came.

As the struggle in America ebbed and flowed, over the succeeding years, Burke contended against the King, the vast majority in Parliament, and predominant public opinion. After two years of fighting, he still demanded a negotiated peace. On April 3, 1777, there was published his *Letter to the Sheriffs of the City of Bristol,* denouncing the ministry's partial suspension of writs of *habeas corpus,* and decrying a war undertaken and conducted without regard for prudence, which with the wise statesman has precedence over right and power. He concluded with a passage on civil liberty which contains the kernel of his understanding of the balance that ought to be maintained between liberty and order. (It is this truth, says Hans Barth, which makes Burke the most important of modern political philosophers.)[11]

> Civil freedom, Gentlemen, is not, as many have endeavored to persuade you, a thing that lies hid in the abstruse science. It is a blessing and a benefit, not an abstract speculation; and all the just reasoning that can be upon it is of so coarse a texture as perfectly to suit the ordinary capacities of those who are to enjoy, and those who are to defend it. Far from any

resemblance to those propositions in geometry and
metaphysics which admit no medium, but must be
true or false in all their latitude, social and civil
freedom, like all other things in common life, are
variously mixed and modified, enjoyed in very different degrees, and shaped into an infinite diversity of
forms, according to the temper and circumstance of
every community. The *extreme* of liberty (which is its
abstract perfection, but its real fault) obtains no-
where, nor ought to obtain anywhere; because ex-
tremes, as we all know, in every point which relates
either to our duties or satisfactions in life, are destructive both to virtue and enjoyment. Liberty, too,
must be limited in order to be possessed. The degree
of restraint it is impossible in any case to settle precisely. But it ought to be the constant aim of every
wise public counsel to find out by cautious experiments, and rational, cool endeavours, with how
little, not how much, of this restraint the community
can subsist; for liberty is a good to be improved, and
not an evil to be lessened.

Ardent though Burke was, all these years, in the advocacy of conciliation and peace, still he had not much
sympathized with the colonists' appeal to alleged natural
right, as embodied by 1776 in the Declaration of Independence. Civil liberty, as suggested in the preceding passage,
is the product of social experience, convention, and compromise, not of an original and unalterable "nature."
Americans were entitled to "the chartered rights of Englishmen"; but they possessed no "natural" right to defy
constitutional authority when it might suit their temporary purposes. Ross Hoffman expresses this point well:

Conciliation of the colonies was to Burke a means rather than an end—a means of preserving the British Empire in North America. The tranquillity and prosperity of the empire formed the object of his politics, not the vindication of natural justice. America was not India: never did Burke imagine that British officials in America were guilty of monstrous tyranny and crimes against the moral law: America was not afflicted by a Warren Hastings. As Burke envisaged the Anglo-American crisis, it was a quarrel brought on by ministerial and parliamentary ignorance and imprudence, inconsistency and imbecile feebleness, which had alienated the natural loyalty of the king's subjects on the other side of the Atlantic.[12]

As Burke had predicted, the American spirit of freedom was not to be crushed. The Rockingham Whigs had been denied their opportunity to effect conciliation while compromise still was possible; they had been ignored in their endeavor to make peace while the Revolution raged. But in 1782, after Cornwallis' troops laid down their arms at Yorktown, the North ministry fell at last. Much though the King disliked the Rockinghams, he was compelled to let the Marquis kiss hands and to permit the second Rockingham ministry to treat with the triumphant Continental Congress. In a victory sufficiently melancholy, Rockingham, Burke, and their friends resumed the government which they had relinquished sixteen years earlier. Meanwhile, an empire had collapsed and a nation had emerged.

4

Reforming Party and Government

James Boswell told a friend that he thought Burke enjoyed continual happiness, if any man might: "He has so much knowledge, so much animation, and the consciousness of so much fame." Yet this was written in 1775, when Burke was endeavoring desperately to stop the fighting in America, and when he was near to collapse from overwork and excess of emotion; when, too, he was at the height of his struggle against the designs of George III, in domestic politics.

"We must find our happiness in work, or not at all." So wrote a twentieth-century admirer of Burke, Irving Babbitt. In the sense that he was perpetually busy with concerns of high—and often enduring—importance, Burke was a happy man. Despite the repeated heavy disappointments he received in politics, a trust in Providence and a certain defiant Irish cheerfulness sustained him. Admired even by his enemies, he had become a power in Parliament, an orator of the first rank, and was known everywhere. His friends were the wisest and liveliest people of the time; his benefactions were many, extending especially to the young painter James Barry and, later, to the poet George Crabbe. For all his lack of money, he lived in a handsome jovial way, justifying Walter Bagehot's observation, in the next century, that "conservatism is enjoyment."

How, indeed, he contrived to carry on simultaneously the immense labors which were his as intellectual leader of the Rockingham Whigs, it is difficult to understand. At the very time he was so deeply involved in American affairs, he also sustained vast responsibilities as the Rockinghams' champion against George III at home, and as the philosopher of conservative reform. His principal lasting achievements in British domestic politics—though transcending England and the age—were his work for responsible party, his definition of the character and duties of a popular representative, and his "Economical Reform" of British government—these occupying much of his time from 1770 to 1782.

"The most crucial political objectives of Burke's career," according to Peter Stanlis, were eight in number:

> (1) To maintain the traditional structure of the British state, centered in divided and balanced powers.
> (2) To define the constitutional limits of the royal prerogative and royal influence.
> (3) To extend the legislative authority of the House of Commons, and maintain the independence of its members.
> (4) To defend the organization and use of political parties as a legitimate and publicly accepted part of the political process.

(5) To extend the civil rights and economic privileges of the British constitution to all British subjects, so far as these are necessary to fulfill the great ends of society—distributive and commutative justice, good order and liberty.

(6) To set forth the principles of sovereignty and civil liberty for the British Empire, by establishing equitable rule between the mother country and all her colonies.

(7) To defend the historical civil order of Europe as a Christian commonwealth, against the scientific materialism and romantic sensibility of the philosophers of the Enlightenment who wished to establish a new social order upon abstract metaphysical theories of man and society.

(8) To combine in all practical problems a complete consideration of historical circumstances, of 'prudence' or expediency on the one hand, with ethical or legal norms on the other.[1]

This present chapter is concerned primarily with the first four of these undertakings. To understand Burke's course of action, it is necessary to glance at his connection with the Rockinghams.

When Lord Rockingham's ministry was dismissed in 1766, Burke at first apparently hoped to obtain office in Grafton's government, and was authorized by Rockingham to do just that; some continuity might be preserved between the Rockingham and Grafton-Pitt governments. After first neglecting Burke because of Pitt's hostility, the ministry approached him through General Conway. But by that time the Rockinghams had split with Chatham and Grafton; and Burke replied to Conway that he would not serve under the Duke of Grafton, since he belonged "not to the administration, but to those who were out": that is, he adhered rigorously to his own concept, then almost fully formulated, of the integrity of political party. From this principle he departed only once, and then only in part—when, in 1783, he entered into short-lived coalition with North and Fox.

The temptation to act otherwise must have been considerable; and no one would have blamed him for it, in those days, had he preferred office to party loyalty. Ross Hoffman speculates on what future Burke might have enjoyed, had he come to terms with Conway in 1766:

> Suppose he had elected for place and kept it after Rockingham had turned against Chatham. That probably would have been a seat on the Board of Trade or the Admiralty Board. His great talents would have been enlisted under Conway and then presumably under North. With such parliamentary abilities as he possessed, up he must have gone, to the Treasury Board, to the Pay Office, to the Exchequer, to an Irish peerage at least. He would have done as well as Gilbert Elliot or Charles Jenkinson, for in the king's service careers were open to talent. With a large and safe salary for a half-sinecure place he might have found the leisure to become the Gibbon of English history; he would have been equal to that.

And public opinion would have sustained him in such a choice:

> Most men thought the way of the placeman right and the way of party wrong. Common opinion held party to mean selfish faction, opposition to the king's min-

isters (if sustained and systematic) to be tainted with disloyalty, and political virtue to consist in serving Majesty in Majesty's appointed way.[2]

Yet Burke chose to side with the coherent opposition almost all his life; and to that choice the whole theory and practice of modern political parties owes much. Rather than writing history, he shaped history. Doubtless Burke's decision was influenced, in part, by that leader of the opposition with whom he had leagued himself—Lord Rockingham. Nowadays historians know much more of Rockingham than once they did. "The Marquis was a man of strong character and large experience in the world," Hoffman writes;

> he knew the courts and kings of Europe, had dined with Roman cardinals, charmed Italian princesses; he spoke three languages, had managed astutely a large fortune, commanded militiamen in war, ruled the politics of Yorkshire, and had been schooled for high public responsibilities by the chiefs of the Whig party. He was their head because they wished it so....[3]

The existence of Rockingham made it possible for Burke to realize—if under heavy handicaps—the concept of responsible party.

In *Thoughts on the Present Discontents* (1770) occurs Burke's chief discussion of the function of party. This was a manifesto of the Rockingham Whigs, but it was more. In essence, it was the first clear exposition of what the "Western democracies" now take for granted as the role of party, organized for the national interest.

Previously, the Whig factions had acted without well-defined principles, governed chiefly by personalities, and interested principally in taking office. Burke meant that the Rockinghams, at least, being the legitimate core of the Whigs, should aspire to something better. George III, he argued, was overthrowing the Constitution by "corruption" (monetary rewards to the King's Friends from the Civil List), and by resorting to a "double cabinet"—that is, in effect ignoring his formal ministry and ruling, actually, through private advisers and servants. The Constitution should be preserved by a party founded on principle, and prepared to spend many years, if necessary, out of office. This party would seek, through frankness and courage, to win the support of popular opinion.

Whether George III actually intended any considerable subversion of the Constitution, and whether he really depended upon a kind of secret cabinet, is still hotly debated among the historians. The school of Sir Lewis Namier looks upon Burke as a mere opportunist, falsely assailing George for the advantage of the Rockinghams; but this view is now giving way, among the major Burke scholars, to a judgment far more favorable.[4] However this may be, the permanent importance of Burke's work for responsible party is not dependent upon the partisan wrangles of that day. The effect of Burke's argument and action was to establish party responsibility; and no British sovereign since George III has ventured to assert to their full extent the powers still theoretically latent in the Crown. In general, the same understanding of the function and duty of political parties has spread to the United States, the British Commonwealth, and other modern states.

"The change Burke promoted was from statesmanship

to party government," Harvey Mansfield, Jr., writes.

> Statesmanship is the capacity to do what is good in
> the circumstances, a capacity in which men, as indi-
> viduals, are variously accomplished. Since they are
> variously accomplished in this, they are unequal; and
> statesmanship is essentially an unequal capacity. As
> such, it must be defined by its best example, not by an
> average sample; for we cannot know what a states-
> man can do unless we know the limit of human
> capacity, that is, what a great man would do. The
> study of statesmanship is therefore chiefly the study
> of great men, and reliance on statesmanship is a
> reliance on the performance and example of great
> men. The replacement of statesmanship by party is an
> attempt to avoid dependence on great men.

Burke was writing about Chatham when he said that acting in a corps tends to reduce the value of a distinguished individual, but he could have been writing about himself. He was a great statesman who sought not merely to reduce Britain's reliance on his single capacity, but to reduce her reliance on the capacity of any great statesman. He promoted this change by introducing parties into the public consti-tution, by making party government the respectable instrument of honest men of principle. Defining 'party' as a body of men united on some particular principle, he made parties available to good men in association against bad men. But a principle on which good men can agree to associate publicly must be an honest principle, a principle which shocks no sensibilities and which sacrifices some of the clear discernment of an 'individual who is of any distin-guished value' to procure the association of good men. It is not that a statesman is unprincipled or above principle; it is rather that his principle loses its refinement in the translation to public speech, and thence to party program.[5]

Yet can one imagine modern Britain, or America, successfully governed by humane statesmen, without the apparatus of party? Burke knew that political parties have their vices. "I do not wonder that the behaviour of many parties should have made persons of tender and scrupulous virtue somewhat out of humour with all sorts of connection in politicks," he wrote in his *Present Discontents.*

> I admit that people frequently acquire in such confederacies a narrow, bigoted, and proscriptive spirit; that they are apt to sink the idea of the general good in this circumscribed and partial interest. But, where duty renders a critical situation a necessary one, it is our business to keep free from the evils attendant upon it; and not to fly from the situation itself.... Commonwealths are made of families, free commonwealths of parties also; and we may as well affirm, that our natural regards and ties of blood tend inevitably to make men bad citizens, as that the bonds of our party weaken those by which we are held to our country.

In Burke's day or ours, parties are imperfect political instruments, necessarily less imaginative than the individual statesman of genius or remarkable talent, and less prompt to act. Yet does it follow that the civil social order has suffered—as Mansfield seems to imply—from the rise of responsible party? The strongest-willed statesman of

England in Burke's time was the elder Pitt, who helped to bring victory in the Seven Years' War; but also Pitt's conduct in the American crisis was eccentric, arbitrary, and conspicuously unsuccessful. If party is a bundle of compromises, at least a well-organized and well-led party knows how to make compromise among great interests possible. The alternative to compromise is, at best, inactivity; and at worst, civil or foreign war.

In the *Discontents* and in his three decades of work with the Rockingham Whigs, Burke labored to develop responsible party because the rising popular interests of his time simply would submit no longer to the ascendancy of court factions or of aristocratic virtue. Responsible party was the alternative to arbitrary rule, or to the ascendancy of demagogue and fanatic. Because the French did not develop coherent parties, governed by prudence, to represent the chief interests in the realm, the French turned to Dr. Guillotin.

"In effect," Mansfield concludes about Burke, "he demoted statesmanship to conservatism." Lord Bolingbroke's aristocratic "men of ability," though surviving because indispensable, today must hide their light beneath the bushel of "responsible" party.

Now truly Burke dreaded the charismatic leader, calling Cromwell "that great bad man." Though himself a "new man," Burke declared that the path to power ought not to be smoothed for men of ability (or, in Burke's phrase, men of "actual virtue"). The presumption and impetuosity of enterprising talents must be checked by "presumptive virtue," the influence of men governed by habit, custom, and a long-instilled sense of duty; such were the country gentlemen—later on, the "fat cattle" squires whom Disraeli led. (During the French Revolution, Burke defined Jacobinism as the revolt of a nation's enterprising talents against its property.) The continuity of a nation's establishments and institutions, the true consensus of many generations, must not be imperiled by the rash innovations of a talented reformer; for though the individual is foolish, the species is wise.

Burke put his trust in prescription, tradition, moral habit, custom—or, as his intellectual heir, T. S. Eliot, expressed it, in the idea of a Christian society, the product of the experience of the species with God and with man in community. (In his first principles, Burke differed profoundly with Bolingbroke, the skeptic, whom Jeffrey Hart calls the chief English disciple of Machiavelli.)[6]

Mansfield implies that somehow Burke opened the way to the politics of rationalism and to the mass society. By his remark that we all must obey the great law of change, and that it is impious to oppose the manifest intention of Providence, Burke (like Tocqueville after him) indeed may have made a breach in the old order. But what was the alternative? Deny a fact, and that fact will be your master. Nineteenth-century liberalism, in large part the creation of Jeremy Bentham, "the great subversive," Burke's most powerful intellectual antagonist, burst like a flood upon the immemorial ways which Burke had defended. Burke, Mansfield writes,

> was able to inspire only one part of the party system with the rules of prudence. His present influence is as a founder of one party, not of the party system. Thus his doctrine of party is now used to tolerate those rationalist 'Jacobins' whom he meant to extirpate.

No doubt. Yet it is vain to oppose a mere theory to an immensely powerful social movement, backed by vast interests. No one understood better than did Burke the futility—nay, the baneful power—of theory divorced from social reality. Without political parties to secure public assent, the English monarchy—even had George III or the Regent enlisted in defense of the Crown a statesman sagacious as Bolingbroke—would have fallen to Jacobin radicalism as did the monarchies of Europe.

The aristocratic domination of Bolingbroke's men of "ability and virtue" was undone by certain material and social forces; so, to a lesser extent, Burke's structure of responsible parties (founded upon a limited electorate) had to give way before new elements in society. Responsible party made it possible for the old and the new in society to come to terms.

One of these innovating forces was military: the development of efficient and cheap firearms, which finally broke Jacobite valor at Culloden, and which presently gave the Parisian mob power to bring down the monarchy or any other regime. (Coming full cycle, today further development of weapons enables twentieth-century governments, enjoying a monopoly of the complex and costly instruments of war in "developed," densely-populated modern countries, to crush in short order any popular rising—as in Hungary, four decades ago; and the authority of King Demos diminishes proportionately in our time.)

Another of these forces was the industrial revolution, transferring wealth and prestige—and with these, power—to classes very different from those influenced by Bolingbroke's and Burke's rhetoric. A third force was the diffusion of literacy and cheap books and newspapers, giving advantage to the "vigorous vulgar rhetoric" of Thomas Paine and his successors.[7] A fourth revolutionary cause was the disintegration of settled community which accompanied the industrial revolution and the abrupt increase of population. And one might list a half-dozen other social hammer-blows against which the old order of governors of the commonwealth could not stand without yielding ground.

Had Burke been more rigorous in his principles, still government by statesmen of the antique pattern would have yielded to the liberal impulse. "Even Mormon counts more votaries than Bentham," Disraeli wrote in the next century. But when the Benthamites had first the new classes and then the new masses at their back, because the material interests of those classes and masses seemed to coincide with Benthamite dogma, necessarily the man of ability and virtue was eclipsed, and new political forms appeared.

Although Bolingbroke and Burke differed upon the role of party, and in part upon the basis of the civil social order, they were not altogether at poles. They held in common these principles (which, in some degree, Burke may have received from Bolingbroke): the concern for futurity which the wise minister has in the forefront of his mind; the need to reconcile opposing groups—but through gradual accommodation; the testing of an alleged consensus by its steadiness over the years, as opposed to "transient fluctuations of feeling."[8] But as for the role of responsible party in modern government, in the long run Burke and his friends defeated Bolingbroke's disciple, George III.

Two decades after publication of the *Present Discontents,* George Washington still looked upon party as baneful faction, and indulged the vain hope that the infant United States might escape such division. But American interests and opinions naturally fell into the embryo party structures of the Federalists and the Republicans; for if party does not exist in a quasi-democratic society, a people must submit to government by an autocrat or an aristocracy— which modern republics will not endure. Burke's party dedicated to the national interest fortunately supplanted parties interested chiefly in the spoils of office—predatory parties of the sort that afflict those "emergent nations" of twentieth-century Africa and Asia which tolerate party at all.

Individuals must submit, in most instances, to the decisions of their party, Burke concluded—though such decisions must be founded upon general principles.

> Men thinking freely, will, in particular instances, think different. But still as the greater part of the measures which arise in the course of public business are related to, or dependent on, some great *leading general principles in Government,* a man must be peculiarly unfortunate in the choice of his political company if he does not agree with them at least nine times in ten. If he does not concur in these general principles upon which the party is founded, and which necessarily draw on a concurrence in their application, he ought from the beginning to have chosen some other, more conformable to his opinions.... How men can proceed without any connexion at all, is to me utterly incomprehensible.[9]

This responsible party upon which Burke relied was aristocratic in its leadership, and founded upon a franchise severely restricted. Burke declared once that the real English nation, in his time, consisted of some four hundred thousand persons—those with some stake in the land, or qualified by education or profession to choose competent members of Parliament and to exercise the functions of local government. He was opposed to wholesale electoral reform unless there was a clear public demand for it; and he discerned no such demand in his own day. Yet he did not desire the total domination of party by the aristocratic interest. As he declared—with true courage for a man allied with Whig magnates—in the *Present Discontents:*

> I am no friend to aristocracy, in the sense at least in which that word is usually understood. If it were not a bad habit to moot cases on the supposed ruin of the constitution, I should be free to declare, that if it must perish, I would rather by far see it resolved into any other form, than lost in that austere and insolent domination.

Eleven years later, in his speech on the bill for repeal of the Marriage Act, he went further into this subject.

> I am accused, I am told abroad, of being a man of aristocratic principles. If by aristocracy they mean the Peers, I have no vulgar admiration, nor any vulgar antipathy, towards them; I hold their order in cold and decent respect. I hold them to be of an absolute necessity in the constitution; but I think they are only good when kept within their proper bounds. I trust, whenever there has been a dispute between these Houses, the part I have taken has not

been equivocal. If by the aristocracy, which indeed comes nearer to the point, they mean an adherence to the rich and powerful against the poor and weak, this would indeed be a very extraordinary part. I have incurred the odium of gentlemen in this House for not paying sufficient regard to men of ample property. When, indeed, the smallest rights of the poorest people in the kingdom are in question, I would set my face against any act of pride and power countenanced by the highest that are in it; and if it should come to the last extremity, and to a contest of blood—God forbid! God forbid!—my part is taken; I would take my fate with the poor, and low, and feeble. But if these people came to turn their liberty into a cloak for maliciousness, and to seek a privilege of exemption, not from power, but from the rules of morality and virtuous discipline, then I would join my hand to make them feel the force which a few, united in a good cause, have over a multitude of the profligate and ferocious.

Parties headed by a Wilkes or a Lord George Gordon, if triumphant, must be the ruin of a commonwealth; such is the fate of factions which exclude any element of the "presumptive virtue" of a nation. In the Rockingham Whigs, Burke endeavored to construct a model of party, headed by men of virtue, though appealing regularly to public opinion. The Rockinghams became, indeed, a body more attached to sound principle, less subject to corruption, and less eager for office, than any faction Britain had known previously. Both the Conservative party and the Liberal party of the latter half of the nineteenth century found in Burke's concept of party responsibility, as in the example of the Rockinghams, the pattern for successful representative government; and American parties, too, felt the influence of Burke.

Still, the Rockingham Whigs could not have prevailed against George III, in his role of "patriot king," except for his defeat in the American war. Acting according to his lights, the King fought at home a battle against the Rockinghams and other Whig factions which he would have won, had it not been for the surrender at Yorktown. "There is something grand about his courage," Thackeray wrote of George III. "He bribed; he bullied; he darkly dissembled on occasion; he exercised a slippery perseverance, which one almost admires, as one thinks his character over. His courage was never to be beat."

The American defeat undid King George and his ministers, for all their obduracy and their clever management. (Burke's Economical Reform, in 1782, greatly diminished the King's power to dominate Parliament through the Civil List.) By March, 1782, the King was compelled to dismiss Lord North and to accept ministers uncongenial to him— an innovation which became an enduring precedent. Lord Rockingham, whom George had tried to ignore when the Marquis had been Prime Minister sixteen years earlier, became again First Lord of the Treasury. The fidelity of the Rockinghams to their principles had been vindicated; and it had been demonstrated that a party can endure exclusion from power for many years, and yet maintain itself for the day of recovery. Burke's ideal of party had taken on flesh.

In the midst of the struggle between the champions of the

supremacy of the House of Commons and the defenders of the royal prerogative—during the period when Burke, his interest in American affairs waning as he gave up the North American colonies for 'ost, bent his energies to the construction of a high-principled party—the Whig "philosopher in action" alienated his popular constituency of Bristol. Thereafter he was to sit, until his resignation from the House of Commons, for a pocket borough. But in this affair of his Bristol seat, as on other occasions, Burke's practical failure produced a manual of political wisdom.

When, in 1774, the merchants and shipowners of Bristol had chosen Burke as one of their members of Parliament, he had given them fair warning that he meant to be their representative, not their mere delegate. In that year, enthusiasts for Wilkes talked much of delegation, rather than representation: a "patriot" in Parliament, they declared, was there to do their immediate bidding. Burke would have no part of that error (though his Bristol colleague, Henry Cruger, supinely promised to be obedient in all things to the will of Bristol). Constituents' wishes should have weight with their member, Burke said; then he added—

> But his own unbiased opinion, his mature judgment, his enlightened conscience, he ought not to sacrifice to you, or to any set of men living. These he does not derive from your pleasure—no, nor from the law and the constitution. They are a trust from Providence, for the abuse of which he is deeply answerable. Your representative owes you, not his industry only, but his judgment; and he betrays, instead of serving you, if he sacrifices it to your opinion.

In a comparatively democratic constituency, this was high ground; and Bristol was not long persuaded to tolerate it. "You choose a member, indeed," Burke had told them;

> but when you have chosen him he is not a member of Bristol, but he is a member of *parliament*. If the local constituent should have an interest or should form a hasty opinion evidently opposite to the real good of the rest of the community, the member for that place ought to be as far, as any other, from any endeavour to give it effect.

Bristol, notwithstanding, continued to think in terms of delegation, ignoring Burke's admonition that Parliament is not a congress of ambassadors, but a deliberative assembly of one nation, concerned with the general good of the nation, and unaffected by local prejudices. The local prejudices of Bristol were very strong. By the autumn of 1777, Burke was aware that he had become unpopular with many men of Bristol, as had the Rockinghams throughout the country. This breach with Bristol widened when Burke—out of his affection for Ireland, and his concern for imperial harmony—supported measures to admit Ireland to free trade with England: that seemed to work against the immediate commercial advantage of Bristol. Though he explained his position to his constituents, he made no concessions.

When, in 1780, the Gordon Riots erupted in London, the Protestant fanatics, backed by the rabble, were especially hot against Burke—for he had supported Sir George Savile's act for the modification of the Penal Laws against Irish Catholics. Here too Burke's friendliness to Catholics and to Ireland went against the grain of many people in Bristol. He was further reproached by some of his constituents for having approved measures for the relief of debtors, and for not having visit ?d Bristol during four years. After suppressing the Gordon Riots, the King issued writs of election, believing the moment to be propitious for the royal interest. Thus Burke found it necessary to go down to Bristol in September, to seek re-election.

His address at the Bristol Guildhall, on September 6, 1780, defending his conduct in Parliament, seems to this writer the most moving and persuasive speech Burke ever uttered. But the Bristol electors, moved by a self-interest not wholly enlightened, thought otherwise.

Burke unflinchingly defended his every stand; he was a member of Parliament for Bristol, not the simple agent of local commercial interests; and he had served Bristol by serving the nation.

"Gentlemen, we must not be peevish with those who serve the people," he said. A forthright member of Parliament should be cherished.

> If we degrade and deprave their minds by servility, it will be absurd to expect, that they who are creeping and abject towards us, will ever be bold and incorruptible assertors of our freedom, against the most seducing and most formidable of all powers. No! human nature is not so formed; nor shall we improve the faculties or better the morals of publick men, by our possession of the most infallible receipt in the world for making cheats and hypocrites.... Where the popular member is narrowed in his ideas, and rendered timid in his proceedings, the service of the crown will be the sole nursery of statesmen.

In advocating justice for Ireland, he continued, he acted in the interest of Britain, as he had acted when he sought conciliation with the Americans. In supporting Lord Beauchamp's bill for the relief of debtors, he regretted only that the bill had not gone far enough, and that it had failed to pass.

As for the Roman Catholics, Savile's Act had secured their loyalty to the nation in a time of dread crisis, and had modified "bad laws...the worst sort of tyranny." Far from promising to amend his views,

> I was never less sorry for any action of my life.... *This way of proscribing the citizens by denominations and general descriptions,* dignified by the name of reason of state, and security for constitutions and common-wealths, is nothing better at bottom, than the miserable invention of an ungenerous ambition which would fain hold the sacred trust of power, without any of the virtues or any of the energies that give a title to it: a receipt of policy, made up of a detestable compound of malice, cowardice, and sloth.... Crimes are the acts of individuals, and not of denominations.

His Guildhall audience scarcely could have been amiable at this moment; but Burke, called "opportunist" by politicians who lived in opulence by subservience to the King, was undeterred. If Bristol would not indulge his conscience, Bristol should not have him:

> When we know, that the opinions of even the greatest multitudes are the standard of rectitude, I shall think myself obliged to make those opinions the masters of my conscience. But if it may be doubted whether Omnipotence itself is competent to alter the

essential constitution of right and wrong, sure I am,
that such *things,* as they and I, are possessed of no
such power. No man carries further than I do the
policy of making government pleasing to the people.
But the widest range of this politick complaisance is
confined within the limits of justice. I would not only
consult the interest of the people, but I would cheer-
fully gratify their humours. We are all a sort of
children that must be soothed and managed. I think
I am not austere or formal in my nature. I would bear,
I would even myself play my part in, any innocent
buffooneries, to divert them. But I never will act the
tyrant for their amusement. If they will mix malice in
their sports, I shall never consent to throw them any
living, sentient, creature whatever, no not so much as
a kitling, to torment.

Being thus stubborn, Burke was told, he might never be
elected to Parliament; and this would be unpleasant.

But I wish to be a member of Parliament, to have my
share of doing good and resisting evil. It would
therefore be absurd to renounce my objects, in order
to gain my seat. I deceive myself indeed most grossly,
if I had not much rather pass the remainder of my life
hidden in the recesses of the deepest obscurity, feed-
ing my mind even with the visions and imaginations
of such things, than to be placed on the most splendid
throne of the universe, tantalized with a denial of the
practice of all which can make the greatest situation
other than the greatest curse. Gentlemen, I have had
my day.

Indeed Burke had. By September 9, it became clear to
him that Bristol did not desire so independent a member as

himself to represent them; they wanted a cunning agent. Declining the poll, he returned to London, and Rockingham found for him the pocket borough of Malton. To the end, the masterful political philosopher, rhetorician, and architect of party represented an obscure safe borough.

Bristol had rejected a man of burning genius, who thought first of justice and of the nation, and second of local electors and local appetites. But Burke's words at Bristol have not been altogether forgotten in Britain or America; and that members of the mother of Parliaments, or of Congress, who still make up their minds little influenced by special interests, lobbyists, and the popular infatuation of the moment—those who give representative government its virtue—may be heartened even today by Burke's intrepidity.

Rejection by Bristol, however, was merely an incident in the sixteen-year-long struggle of the Rockinghams to restrain the King's ambition and to accomplish a moderate reform of government. Here we return to the thread of that political labyrinth.

In 1782, George III found it necessary to accept Lord Rockingham as Prime Minister, though the King saddled Rockingham with Lord Shelburne as Secretary for Colonial and Irish Affairs. After sixteen lean years, Burke obtained the triumph of his principles (though a melancholy victory, the result of military defeat in America); also he obtained once more a place in government.

Entering upon a second brief tenure of office, Burke was appointed Paymaster to the Forces—not the most lofty of posts, but a highly lucrative one. It had been custom for the

Paymaster to be permitted to lend out at interest, for his private profit, monies which his office had temporarily on hand. This privilege had given previous Paymasters an annual income of perhaps twenty-three thousand pounds; Rigby, a member of the Bedford gang, had accumulated half a million pounds from his tenure of this place. With a fidelity to his principles astonishing in the eighteenth century, Burke promptly reduced the perquisites of his own office—despite his need of money—by abolishing the privilege of lending funds and fixing the salary at a mere four thousand pounds. "In view of this," Bertram Newman comments, "to inquire unfavourably into the efforts which Burke made from time to time to obtain offices for himself and his relations, is surely the refinement of pedantry."[10]

The Rockinghams had to make peace with the Americans and their European allies; also they now found opportunity to introduce the reforms of government they had so long advocated as voices in the wilderness. Their chief practical accomplishment was Burke's long-demanded "Economical Reform."

In 1780, Burke had first introduced his bill for reform of the Crown's Civil List, abolishing obsolete or useless offices, diminishing royal political power exercised through the grant of pensions or through secret-service funds, and asserting the control of Parliament over what is now called the civil service. His mastery of detail impressed even the hostile majority in the House of Commons. He would have postponed the Reform indefinitely, Burke said, were it to work injustice upon a single tidewaiter (customs officer); but he had drawn up a bill which would respect all legitimate claims. In his "Speech on the Economical Reform," he distinguished between temperate and hot reform: genuine reform, to avoid new abuses, must be accomplished gradually, the reformer "sounding the lead every inch of the way," as Burke put it later. "If I cannot reform with equity, I will not reform at all," he declared in 1780.

A government with an annual deficit of fourteen million pounds required the prompt attention of the reformer, nevertheless. It was neither too early nor too late to commence:

> Early reformations are amicable arrangements with a friend in power; late reformations are terms imposed upon a conquered enemy: early reformations are made in cool blood; late reformations are made under a state of inflammation. In that state of things the people behold in government nothing that is respectable. They see the abuse, and they will see nothing else. They fall into the temper of a furious populace provoked at the disorder of a house of ill fame; they go to work by the shortest way: they abate the nuisance, they pull down the house.

Burke meant to eliminate the sinecures by which the King rewarded obedient members of Parliament; he meant to reduce extravagance and satisfy the popular demand for economy, at the same time paying the heavy arrears of the Civil List; he meant to work an enduring improvement of the government. But he did not confound retrenchment and niggardliness. As he expressed it in the impressive "Speech on the Economical Reform":

> Mere parsimony is not economy. It is separable in

theory from it; and, in fact, it may, or may not, be a *part* of economy, according to circumstances. Expense, and great expense, may be an essential part in true economy. If parsimony were to be considered as one of the kinds of that virtue, there is, however, another and a higher economy. Economy is a distributive virtue, and consists not in saving but in selection. Parsimony requires no providence, no sagacity, no comparison, no judgment. Mere instinct, and that not of the noblest kind, may produce this false economy in perfection. The other economy has larger views. It demands a discriminating judgment, and a firm, sagacious mind.

With some reluctant agreement, even King's Friends and Tories listened respectfully to Burke's calm description of the abuse of the Civil List. Edward Gibbon, sitting in the House of Commons with a sinecure to secure his vote for Lord North, confessed that he trembled while he admired Burke, in "the delight with which that diffusive and ingenious orator Mr. Burke was heard, and even by those whose existence he proscribed." For all that, Parliament twice rejected Burke's reform.

By 1782, however, public opinion so insistently demanded retrenchment and improvement of the Civil List that a modified version of Burke's bill passed into law on July 11. One of its more valuable features was the ordering and classification of Civil List payments. Parliament was thus established as the supervisor and regulator of "patronage" and the civil service; the King's power of "corruption" was vastly reduced, though he retained—and subsequently exercised to the full—the power to create new peers, thus assuring his control over the House of Lords.

The modern British civil service, the most efficient in the world, has roots in Burke's reform.

As Ross Hoffman remarks, Burke was a reforming conservative, rather than a conservative reformer. "He wished to reform in order to conserve."[11] When no pressing need for alteration was discernible, it was best to endure existing abuses rather than to invite, by imprudent tinkering, new evils less easily endured. Innovation, Burke argued, is not synonymous with reform. Thus he set his face against most proposals for the reform of Parliament, even though he acknowledged that absurdities and anomalies existed in parliamentary representation. In his "Speech on the Economical Reform," he had observed that the preservation of the ancient merely because of its antiquity can produce absurdities:

> It is to burn precious oils in the tomb; it is to offer meat and drink to the dead—not so much an honour to the deceased, as a disgrace to the survivors.... They put me in mind of *Old Sarum,* where the representatives, more in number than the constituents, only serve to inform us, that this was once a place of trade, and sounding with 'the busy hum of men,' though now you can only trace the streets by the colour of the corn; and its sole manufacture is in members of parliament.

Yet radical reformation—even of the rotten borough of Old Sarum—might destroy the curious edifice of the English Constitution, incongruous in the parts of its architecture, yet holding together durably—so long as ambitious architects did not try to make it harmonious, and by tampering bring down the roof. Therefore Burke opposed

Fox's demand, in 1780, for annual parliaments and a hundred new constituencies in the counties, to break royal influence over Parliament. Frequent elections, Burke replied, would produce Parliamentary confusion and (by the costs) the ruin of independent members.

And two years later, he refused to support the younger Pitt's bill for a redistribution of seats in the Commons, revision of constituencies, and admission of more electors to the rolls. The House of Commons had grown through English history; the attempt to make it symmetrical, to convert it into an abstract mathematical representation of people told by the head, would only bring the House into disrepute and discredit with the people. There exists a legitimate presumption, he said, in favor of things long established:

> It is a presumption in favour of any settled scheme of government against any untried project that a nation has long existed and flourished under it. It is a better presumption even of the *choice* of a nation— far better than any sudden and temporary arrangement by actual election. Because a nation is not an idea only of local extent and individual momentary aggregation, but it is an idea of continuity which extends in time as well as in numbers and in space. And this is a choice not of one day or one set of people, not a tumultuary and giddy choice; it is a deliberate election of ages and of generations; it is a constitution made by what is ten thousand times better than choice: it is made by the peculiar circumstances, occasions, tempers, dispositions, and moral, civil, and social habitudes of the people, which disclose themselves only in a long space of time. It is a vestment

which accommodates itself to the body. Nor is prescription of government formed upon blind, un-
meaning prejudices. For man is a most unwise and a
most wise being. The individual is foolish; the multitude, for the moment, is foolish, when they act without deliberation; but the species is wise, and when
time is given to it, as a species, it almost always acts
right.

Burke's opportunity for effective reform was brief, and
he entered upon even administrative alteration with a
confessed reluctance; yet he knew that "change is the
means of our preservation," and he acted accordingly, so
far as lay in his power. "I look with filial reverence on the
constitution of my country," he concluded his speech of
May 17, 1782, against Pitt's proposed reform of representation,

and never will cut it into pieces, and put it into the
kettle of any magician, in order to boil it, with the
puddle of their compounds, into youth and vigour.
On the contrary, I will drive away such pretenders; I
will nurse its venerable age, and with lenient arts
extend a parent's breath.

These "lenient arts" were measures of improvement
consonant with prudence, social continuity, and prescription. Francis Canavan summarizes Burke's work as an
improver of the civil social order:

It is clear that he was not an arch-conservative or a
reactionary. Rather, he was a classic figure of the
moderate reformer: intensely aware of the complex
and problematical nature of social reality, distrust-

ful of abstract and idealistic demands that justice be done though the heavens should fall, yet willing to remedy concrete abuses with practical measures, concerned always to conserve as well as to improve, and, therefore, cautious and pragmatic even when most resolute in advocating reform. Whether such a man can be an effective reformer is a question of more than academic interest to a generation living in today's revolutionary world. I shall claim no more for Burke than that even radicals can learn wisdom from him, though it should serve only to make them more intelligent radicals.[12]

In 1782, as he had in 1766, Burke presumably looked forward to a considerable period in office, during which the House of Commons, Rockingham being Prime Minister, might accomplish prudent improvements in Irish affairs, the Indian Empire, the relationship between Crown and Parliament, the restoration of friendly relations with America and France, and many other fields—as they just had done in governmental administration. Secure in his party and his place, he enjoyed the prospect of some leisure at last.

Then, abruptly, amidst difficulties about peace with America and graver troubles in Ireland, the Marquis of Rockingham died in office, on July 1, 1782. The King promptly chose Lord Shelburne as Rockingham's successor. Confused and temporarily leaderless, the Rockinghams abandoned office—though Burke, who detested Shelburne, would have had them cling to power in defiance of the King.

Resigning his office of Paymaster and his salary, Burke once more fell upon hard days. The Duke of Portland gradually marshaled the disheartened Rockinghams; and negotiations commenced—initially opposed by Burke— for resuming power through a coalition. As this took form, Lord North and the Portland Whigs (formerly the Rockinghams), with Charles James Fox as the principal mover among them, made common cause against Shelburne and the King. Burke presently acquiesced, reluctantly—and at length embraced the Coalition as a necessity which might permit his party to restrain the King and resume Whig measures.

From its commencement in the spring of 1783, nevertheless, the Fox-North Coalition was subjected to public ridicule and abuse. Much of this was unjustified, for, as Carl Cone observes, the real barrier between North and the Rockinghams was removed by the triumph of the Americans.

> The coalition of North and the Portland party was one of the three available alternatives in 1783 and the most harmonious one. The differences between North and the Portland party on parliamentary reform, on the constitution and the prerogative, as well as on personal relationships, were much less pronounced than the differences between either of them and the Shelburne party.[13]

Yet the Coalition was ill-fated from the first. Burke resumed the post of Paymaster to the Forces, and was more important now than he had been in the Rockingham ministry; indeed, with Fox and North, he was a member of a triumvirate, with Portland as nominal Prime Minister. (Burke's lack of large fortune and great family connections denied him, now as earlier, any important cabinet post;

besides, his Whig colleagues seem to have thought him too impulsive to serve well in such an administrative station, valuable though his passionate talents were in the House). The Shelburne interest, the Chathamites, and lesser parliamentary groups constantly assailed the Coalition as unnatural and unscrupulously eager for place; the British public remembered only too well that at the height of the American crisis, Burke had demanded North's impeachment, and Fox had cried that North should be put to death for high treason; the King detested his ministers.

After eighteen months of existence, the Coalition was brought down by troubles in India. North, Fox, and Burke had been endeavoring to maintain the independence of Parliament against the royal prerogative. Though George III commanded the support only of a minority in the House of Commons, he had won again, and the younger Pitt became his Prime Minister in December, 1784.

The Tory party had risen from the ashes. Edmund Burke—who had not much enjoyed his ministerial post, aside from its salary—was back in the opposition. There he would remain until the Whigs were riven in two, and so long as he held a seat in the Commons.

5

India and Justice

Some sixteen years Burke devoted, above all else, to Indian affairs and the prosecution of Warren Hastings—the period when, in his own words, "I laboured with the most assiduity and met with the least success." At the end, Hastings went free—and was rewarded by a pension somewhat larger than that allotted to Burke about the same time.

Yet British rule in India took on a better character thereafter, and Burke's eloquence contributed much to the pattern of English imperial administration which endured—though vastly diminished—until recent times. Still more important, Burke expressed principles of justice, universal in their application, that have lost nothing with the passing of the years.

Although Burke never visited India (nor went farther abroad than France) he acquired by study, correspondence, and conversation a prodigious knowledge of the subcontinent of which only the kernel appears in the many volumes of his works concerned with Indian matters. Until

1780, he did not address himself systematically to the subject; but thereafter, he made India his principal interest until the French Revolution was well advanced.

British India, from Burke's childhood until Pitt's India Act of 1784, was governed not directly by the British Crown, but by the East India Company, "John Company." In most of the territories under its control, this mercantile corporation kept up the pretense that it acted as agent for the decayed power of the Mogul Empire. Clive's victories during the Seven Years' War had terminated the threat of the French in India; from that triumph onward, the contest was between the East India Company and the Indian princes and peoples. By what principles of law and equity ought the Company to rule its Indian domain? How far was the Company subject to Crown and Parliament, thousands of miles distant? Such questions began to arise during Burke's early years in the House of Commons.

Until 1780, Burke and the Rockinghams generally were friendly toward the East India Company. In 1766, the Rockinghams began to defend the Company against interference by the ministry, which had introduced a bill of dubious sincerity meant primarily to extract revenue from the Company. Looking upon this as an invasion of chartered rights, the Rockinghams fought fiercely—though unsuccessfully—against the measure. In 1772, Burke opposed a parliamentary investigation into the Company's past affairs, believing this proposal to be malignly punitive.

Knowing Burke for a friend, that same year the Company invited him to serve as chairman of a committee of supervisors who would visit India and put the Company's confused business in order; he would have been paid the princely annual salary of ten thousand pounds. But the Rockinghams needing him at home, Burke declined, despite his lack of an adequate income.

By 1773, when North's Regulating Act for India was adopted, Burke's close attention to Indian affairs had convinced him that the Governor-General of Bengal, Warren Hastings, ought to be scrutinized with suspicion. Reports of corruption and arbitrary abuse of power by the Company's servants could not be dismissed; and Burke thought that Hastings, set upon so grand an eminence, might be at the bottom of the infamy. This attitude probably was strengthened in Burke's mind, during the next few years, by the correspondence of Philip Francis (the reputed author of the mordant *Letters of Junius,* often mistakenly attributed to Burke himself), whom Burke had known slightly before Francis went out to India as one of the four members of the Council of Bengal appointed under North's Regulating Act. Fearless, able, and ruthlessly ambitious, Francis meant to supplant Hastings as master of India; baffled in this, he fought a duel with Hastings, was wounded, and returned to England (late in 1780) to become Burke's close friend and a prime mover in the impeachment of Hastings.[1]

Information about another quarter of India came to Edmund Burke from his kinsman William, who went out to Madras in 1777, employed by friends of Lord Pigot to obtain Pigot's freedom. (He had been illegally imprisoned by the Nawab of Arcot, in collusion with his enemies in the Council of Madras.) Although Pigot died in confinement before Will Burke reached Madras, while in India the adventurous and speculative Will obtained appointment as

London agent of the Rajah of Tanjore, who had been wronged by the Nawab of Arcot. Returning to England in 1778, Will reinforced Edmund's previous belief that Hastings was involved in the notoriously prevalent tyranny and extortion of the sub-continent, including the Pigot affair.

Even without the urging of Philip Francis and William Burke, however, Edmund Burke doubtless would have looked upon the conduct of the East India Company's agents as outrageous. Precisely as he had contended against the abuse of British power in America and Ireland, now he took up the cause of justice in India. Today no reputable historian denies that the East India Company, as its territories and power grew, had become incapable of governing well an empire acquired almost in a fit of absence of mind: many of its servants, intent upon making immense fortunes in a few years, ignored the laws of the Indian principalities and peoples, the laws of England, and the principles of natural justice.

Warren Hastings was a better man—and an abler—than his subordinates; but in time Burke's indignation fastened upon Hastings as the nominal superior of all the East India Company's holdings. Hastings had saved British India from destruction by its enemies, and—by comparison with many others—had been modest (though arbitrary) in his extracting of a fortune from the people he governed. Yet if not personally greedy, still Hastings had resorted to measures of money-raising and repression of all opponents which no system of jurisprudence would justify. Probably Hastings could not be punished (for one thing, the House of Commons already was sprinkled with East India "nabobs" and their friends, who had bought parliamentary seats with part of their loot); yet Hastings, as symbol of lawless power, might be discredited and rebuked; and thus a reform of British authority in India might be advanced.

But this is to anticipate. Burke was given opportunity to press for such a reform when, in 1781, he was appointed to a "Select Committee" of the House of Commons to investigate alleged injustices in Bengal, the war with Hyder Ali, and other Indian difficulties; at the same time, the House appointed a "Secret Committee," headed by Henry Dundas, to look into similar matters. Although as yet Burke was not inveterately hostile to Hastings, he sternly opposed the wars against the Marathas and the Rohillas in which Hastings, as the Company's grand servant, had involved British power.

These committees' reports—two of them written by Burke—caused the House of Commons to demand that the Indian princes be assured Britain would not make war upon them, and that the Company recall Hastings to England (which the directors of the Company declined to do). Burke and his friends, going farther, by this time were resolved that the East India Company should be reduced to its original commercial functions; only by such a measure might order and justice be restored to India. And Hastings must be punished.

On April 25, 1782—while in office under Lord Rockingham—Burke wrote to his kinsman Will that Henry Dundas, an eminent member of the Opposition and chairman of the Secret Committee on India, was proceeding famously in the investigation of Hastings' conduct, particularly in the struggle between the Nawab of Arcot and the Rajah of Tanjore:

> His speeches, as well as his Resolutions relative to
> Tanjour, and the oppressions and usurpations of the
> Nabob, were such, as if your own honest heart had
> dictated them. He has not yet brought out the whole,
> but he will bring forward such on Monday next, as
> will free that unfortunate Prince, and harassed Coun-
> try from the wicked Usurpation of Mr. Hastings.[2]

Charles James Fox and Edmund Burke were as one in
this plan. On coming to power in the Coalition of 1783, Fox
introduced his bills—in which Burke had a large hand—
for appointing government commissioners to assume the
Company's political powers. Though reluctant to interfere
with the charter of a private company, Burke argued that
the enormous abuse of the Company's authority and
opportunities now had made it imperative that Parliament
intervene: the "chartered rights of men," or the complex of
liberties, privileges, and immunities which men (including
Indians) had acquired through the growth of a society,
took precedence over company charters.

Fox's reforming bills failed to pass, in part because Fox
was suspected of meaning to usurp the Crown's prerogative of appointment to office where Indian posts were
concerned. This defeat was the immediate cause of the fall
of the Coalition.

Burke's speech (December 1, 1783) on Fox's East India
Bill, nevertheless, defies the tooth of time, containing the
gist of Burke's sixteen-year contest against the Company
and Hastings. Englishmen were exploiting the Indian peoples
to the ruin of India and the disgrace of British justice, Burke

thundered: Providential retribution, perhaps in the form of expulsion from India, must be expected, unless prompt amendment be made—and punishment meted out to malefactors. English rule was worse than the Tartar tyranny; for the Tartars settled down in India, so that their ferocity was diminished by self-interest; while the agents of the Company, intent only upon prompt plunder, were reducing whole kingdoms to abject and permanent poverty:

> The Tartar invasion was mischievous; but it is our protection that destroys India. It was their enmity, but it is our friendship. Our conquest there, after twenty years, is as crude as it was the first day. The natives scarcely know what it is to see the grey head of an Englishman. Young men (boys almost) govern there, without society, and without sympathy with the natives. They have no more social habits with the people, than if they still resided in England; nor indeed any species of intercourse but that which is necessary to making a sudden fortune, with a view to a remote settlement. Animated by all the avarice of age, and all the impetuosity of youth, they roll in one after another; wave after wave; and there is nothing before the eyes of the natives but an endless, hopeless prospect of new flights of birds of prey and passage, with appetites continually renewing for a food that is continually wasting. Every rupee of profit made by an Englishman is lost for ever to India. With us are no retributory superstitions, by which a foundation of charity compensates, through ages, to the poor, for the rapine and injustice of a day. With us no pride erects stately monuments which repair the mischiefs

which pride has produced, and which adorn a country out of its own spoils. England has erected no churches, no hospitals, no palaces, no schools; England has built no bridges, made no high roads, cut no navigations, dug out no reservoirs. Every other conqueror of every other description has left some monument, either of state or beneficence, behind him. Were we to be driven out of India this day, nothing would remain to tell that it had been possessed, during the inglorious period of our domination, by any thing better than the orangoutang or the tiger.

Returning to England, the authors of this devastation use their booty to secure influence and political power—so Burke went on.

In India all the vices operate by which sudden fortune is acquired; in England are often displayed by the same persons the virtues which dispense hereditary wealth. Arrived in England, the destroyers of the nobility and gentry of a whole kingdom will find the best company in this nation, at a board of elegance and hospitality. Here the manufacturer and the husbandman will bless the just and punctual hand that in India has torn the cloth from the loom, or wrested the scanty portion of rice and salt from the peasant of Bengal, or wrung from him the very opium in which he forgot his oppressions and his oppressor. They marry into your families; they enter into your senate; they ease your estates by loans; they raise their value by demand; they cherish and protect your relations which lie heavy on your patronage; and there is scarcely a house in the kingdom that does not feel

some concern and interest that makes all reform of
our eastern government appear officious and dis-
gusting; and on the whole, a most discouraging attempt. In such an attempt you hurt those who are
able to return kindness, or resist injury. If you succeed, you save those who cannot so much as give you
thanks.

When the East India bills were rejected by the House of
Lords, and the Coalition fell from power, Burke, Fox,
Richard Brinsley Sheridan, and the other advocates of
Indian reform had to carry on their fight in opposition,
with faint prospect of success. But a Tory reform was in
process. Pitt now was Prime Minister; he and Dundas drew
up and succeeded in passing Pitt's India Act, which incor-
porated some of the provisions of Fox's and Burke's bill,
though in a disguised form. Pitt and Dundas found it
prudent to leave the formidable Hastings untouched personally—though Hastings detested the India Act. And
Burke could not abide Hastings' immunity.

The House of Commons elected in 1784 was far less
friendly to Burke than that in which he had sat previously;
but he meant to persuade the members that there existed
a legitimate presumption of Hastings' guilt—in which
endeavor the evidence was on Burke's side. On July 30,
1784, before a hostile House, he laid his hand on one of the
seventeen volumes of reports of his Select Committee, and
told the country gentlemen who in those times made up
the big majority of the House:

I swear by this book, that the wrongs done to
humanity in the eastern world, shall be avenged on
those who have inflicted them. They will find, when

the measure of their iniquity is full, that Providence is not asleep. The wrath of Heaven will sooner or later fall upon a nation, that suffers, with impunity, its rulers thus to oppress the weak and innocent. We had already lost one empire, perhaps, as a punishment for the cruelties authorized in another. And men might exert their ingenuity in qualifying facts as they pleased, but there was only one standard by which the Judge of all the earth would try them. It was not whether the interest of the East India Company had made them necessary, but whether they coincided with the prior interests of humanity, of substantial justice, with those rights which were paramount to all others.

Clearly, Burke now had passed far beyond those politicians who advocated an inquiry into the affairs of the Company and the conduct of Hastings merely for partisan or private advantage. He was intent upon punishment of oppressors and peculators in India. The general argument against his demand for justice was that the laws of Britain did not run in India, and that the necessity of raising funds to maintain British security there, with the absence of order in the crumbling and shadowy Mogul Empire, must excuse much that would not be tolerated in Britain. Even Will Burke, back in Madras (still seeking a fortune, but making only a bad name for himself) wrote to young Richard, Edmund's son: "The English here are a respectable, humane, friendly people, nor can I for the Soul of me feel as your father does for the Black Primates." Was it necessary to alienate Englishmen of high influence in order to bring to those who never had known it equity among themselves—to these rascally natives of Madras?

"Do say for me to your father that the abstract right of things in the East has scarcely an existence; all is Usurpation and Force."[3]

For Edmund Burke, however, the first principles of morality were not mere relative matters of geography. He did recognize the immense diversity of social institutions and customs; yet he knew that, although in our Father's house there are many mansions, not all of these are upon the same floor. Apprehending as they did the postulates of distributive and commutative justice, the English masters of India would be false to their duty if they should excuse their own transgressions by pointing to the violent or fraudulent ways of the people among whom they had established themselves.

Will Burke had in mind, no doubt, the dramatic speech which Edmund had delivered in February, 1785, on the Nawab (or Nabob) of Arcot's debts. Hastings had used the profligate Nabob as a tool for extracting money to fill the pockets of the East India Company's servants—and, like other exactions from native princes or their subjects, to pay for military campaigns. To find the rupees, the Nabob had invaded Tanjore and had planned the conquest of the more powerful state of Mysore. This had waked the wrath of the dreadful Hyder Ali, ruler of Mysore, who had retaliated by devastating the Carnatic, from which the Nabob of Arcot drew his mortgaged revenue. Thus were the East India Company and British forces drawn further into Indian military adventures.

More, at least thirteen members of Parliament were among the Nabob's happy creditors, enriched by usurious interest extracted from his unfortunate subjects of the

Carnatic; these and others supported Hastings in his policies; indeed, Pitt and Dundas had been induced to soften their attitude toward Hastings, that they might secure the parliamentary support of Paul Benfield, one of the most notorious of the men who had profited by the spoil of India, and who controlled a bloc of parliamentary constituencies. Corruption in India thus was converted into corruption in England, Burke repeated. This notable speech is the most successful endeavor ever made to transmute the dusty matter of finance into an incandescent phenomenon of the moral imagination.

Meanwhile, the other chief principal in this tragic drama, Warren Hastings, had resigned his governor-generalship and prepared to return to England, where he expected to take up a dignified and affluent retirement on the estate of his ancestors (restored by him at heavy expense). Hastings assumed that his would be a triumphal entry into London. Instead, Burke had prepared Hastings' impeachment. Landing in England in June, 1785, Hastings found himself the subject of a grim parliamentary inquiry—and soon a prisoner before the bar.

From the first, Burke knew that he could not succeed in securing the conviction of the Governor-General; he undertook the impeachment only as a means to rouse Parliament and the public against the oppression of India. "We know that we bring before a bribed tribunal a prejudged cause," he wrote to Philip Francis on December 10, 1785.

> In that situation all that we have to do is to make a case strong in proof and in importance, and to draw inferences from it justifiable in logick, policy and

criminal justice.... Speaking for myself, my business is not to consider what will convict Mr. Hastings (a thing we all know to be impracticable) but what will acquit and justify myself to those few persons and to those distant times, which may take a concern in these affairs and the Actors in them.[4]

In the twentieth century, several historians have impeached Burke, rather than Hastings—asserting that Burke acted from partisan or private motives. But the closest study of Burke on Indian matters has been made by Carl Cone, who acquits Burke of such imputations:

Burke possessed a rich imagination and warm humanitarian concern for all who suffered or seemed to suffer from oppression. Once aroused, his nature would not let him stop. The difference between him and all others who were concerned in the business of India and Hastings was measured by his deeper passion and his greater ability to desire intensely the well-being of humanity.[5]

It is not possible here to enter into the wondrous complexity of the charges against Hastings. Among the principal of these were the allegations that he had doubled the tribute levied upon Cheyt Singh, Rajah of Benares, so driving that prince into rebellion; besting the Rajah, Hastings had deposed him and extracted the immense tribute from his successor. Next, Hastings was accused of confiscating the treasure of the widowed Begums of Oudh, after treating the captive princesses with indignity and tormenting their servants. (The dramatist Richard Brinsley Sheridan spoke on this charge, with theatrical effect, on

February 7, 1787.) In addition, Hastings was charged with a whole series of violations of treaties, misappropriation of funds, robberies, and acts of corruption.

Hastings' best biographer, Keith Feiling, though he defends the Governor-General on nearly all counts, and for all his contempt for Burke in this undertaking, concedes that Hastings' policy in Oudh did at least come close to "political crime."[6] Volume after volume of Burke's collected works contains the descriptions of Hastings' highhanded acts, fascinating reading still; but a bald recital of Indian politics and war in the eighteenth century would be tedious here, even were there space for it.

Hastings' defense, generally speaking, was that he possessed "arbitrary power" to do as he thought best, with no limits imposed by Company or Crown; that he had acted always for the best interest of Britain and of the Company; and that his alleged "spoliations" had been fines levied upon rebels, or abettors of rebellion, to provide for the defense of British India. Should he not be rewarded, rather than punished, as the architect of victory?

In an astounding parliamentary triumph, Burke and his colleagues prevailed upon the House of Commons—despite the backing which the King and the East India Company gave to Hastings—to vote for impeachment. On April 3, 1787, without a division, the House agreed to nine of the twenty-two charges brought against Hastings. Burke, Fox, Sheridan, William Windham, and Sir Gilbert Elliot were chosen to frame the articles of impeachment before the House of Lords. It would be another eight years before the Lords handed down their verdict.

Burke's case against Hastings was founded upon an

understanding of the natural moral law. The Governor-General had ridden rough-shod over the native laws of the Indians; he had considered himself not bound, in Bengal, by English statutes or English customs. Hastings in office was, indeed, not clearly required to observe any particular system of positive law, and so it would have been difficult to convict him of violating what he never had been instructed to respect. But Burke's principal argument was that Hastings had set at defiance the first principles of justice, universally true, which no governor may ignore and yet be guiltless.

Hastings had declared boldly that he possessed, in India, "arbitrary power"; in a letter to Pitt, late in 1784, he had contended that his power could not be "too despotic" for maintaining the British interest in the sub-continent. In his speech (February 16, 1788) on the fourth day of the trial before the House of Lords, Burke replied that no man rightfully can exercise arbitrary power.

All power is of God, and the East India Company, the King, the House of Lords, and the House of Commons have no arbitrary power—no limitless authority—to confer, "because arbitrary power is a thing, which neither any man can hold or any man can give. No man can lawfully govern himself according to his own will, much less can any one person be governed by the will of another." Not the private will, but the law, maintains the internal order of the soul and the external order of society.

When dealing with European affairs, Burke ordinarily had referred to the "law of nations," the legal usages of Europe, derived from Christianity, the remains of Roman civil law, and Germanic customary law. These sources, of course, did not constitute justice in India. But also Burke looked upon the "law of nations" as drawn from the natural law—that is, from the principles of justice which we perceive as natural to the human condition, and which have been ordained by God for man.[7] As Peter Stanlis observes,

> He certainly believed that the Natural Law applied equally in India and in England; he admitted that Hastings had brought disgrace upon Britain's honor by violating the law of nations in Asia, and he stated that Cheyt Singh, in refusing to pay tribute to Hastings, was justifiable upon every principle of the laws of nations, nature, and morality.[8]

So Burke, asking the Lords to find Hastings guilty of high crimes and misdemeanors, expounded the Ciceronian and Christian doctrines of the natural law. "We are all born in subjection," he continued,

> all born equally, high and low, governours and governed, in subjection to one great, immutable, pre-existent law, prior to all our devices, and prior to all our contrivances, paramount to all our ideas, and all our sensations, antecedent to our very existence, by which we are knit and connected in the eternal frame of the Universe, out of which we cannot stir.

That the British in eighteenth-century India, during and after the Seven Years' War, had ruled unjustly, for the gain of voracious adventurers, is denied by few nowadays. But perhaps Burke weakened his "crusade" by concentrating his attack upon Warren Hastings. The Governor-General was by no means guiltless; yet lesser officials had done

worse things, and the affairs of Madras were more lamen-
table than those of Bengal, over which Hastings had held
direct authority. Of some charges against him, Hastings
was quite—or virtually—innocent; others could not be
proved in a court of law; and for the rest, Hastings'
apologists pleaded "necessities of state"—for state necessity proverbially knows no law—though Hastings himself,
at least during his trial, disdained this plea. Hastings'
administrative responsibility for all Indian affairs (though
his actual power had been something less), however—and
his arrogance—made the Governor-General, for Burke,
an almost diabolical source of every Indian affliction.

For more than seven years—1788 to 1795—the trial
before the Lords dragged on, even if the result was fore-
gone. (The House of Lords sat to try the case only a limited
number of days in each year, ranging from thirty-five days
in 1788 to three days in 1794.) As principal manager for the
House of Commons' prosecution, Burke was consumed by
the endeavor—which coincided, presently, with his battle
against the French Revolution. Although often carried
away by his own intemperate invective, and fighting against
hopeless odds, Burke persevered to the end. Even some of
those who had applauded him into this ferocious controversy lost heart, and would have persuaded him to desist.

He would not yield. For Hastings' offenses, he was
convinced, constituted an attack on the whole social fabric
of India, and worked to dissolve the moral and customary
bonds which unite men for the common good. Breaking
down old custom, prescription, habit, and authority in
India, Hastings—or men of Hastings' arrogant stamp—
would be the reckless authors of revolution and anarchy,

as reaction against tyranny. English errors or injustices in America and Ireland were very small, if set against the misgovernment of India. Francis Canavan puts this point well:

> Burke's denunciation of Warren Hastings was made on the same principle as his indictment of the French Revolution. He accused Hastings of holding that the people of India had no rights against their government. But the terms in which this accusation was made are significant. Burke said [in the trial of Hastings, May 28, 1794]: 'The people, he [Hastings] asserts, have no liberty, no laws, no inheritance, no fixed property, no descendable estate, no subordinations in society, no sense of honour, or of shame.'... Burke recurred to principles of natural law in his attack on Hastings' administration of India. Yet he did not conceive the rights of which he accused Hastings of depriving the people of India as naked natural rights. Rather, the rights and liberties of the Indian people are spoken of here as dependent on a society structured by rank and property, ordered by law, and supported by sentiments of honor and shame.[9]

Hastings' acts, that is, amounted to a kind of treason against "the chartered rights of men" (something very different from Thomas Paine's *Rights of Man*). Every society develops such rights through its historic experience; the form of such rights will vary from one people to another, but their source is Providential intent; through these rights, man becomes truly human; the oppressor, depriving men of rights, dehumanizes men. Hastings had flouted what Burke later called "the contract of eternal society," joining God and man, and linking together the dead, the living, and those yet unborn. The economic harm which British rule did to India by discouraging manufactures for the sake of producing exportable raw materials was nothing by the side of the damage being worked by reckless dissolution of the bonds of community. The East India Company, though its purpose was mercantile, still had the gravest moral and social responsibilities in its territories. As Burke had said in the debate on Fox's East India bills, it was no easy task for the British to govern well in India:

> All these circumstances are not, I confess, very favourable to the idea of our attempting to govern India at all. But there we are; there we are placed by the Sovereign Disposer; and we must do the best we can in our situation. The situation of man is the preceptor of his duty.

Burke knew that every society, if one pokes deep enough into its origins, has foundations in revolution or conquest; we draw a "sacred veil" over the beginnings of sovereignty. He did not expect Hastings, a conqueror, to behave in India as an officer of the Crown would behave in England. But there are limits to even the authority of a founder of empire; and Hastings had been subverting, rather than establishing, that balance of order and freedom in which justice may be known. "Law and Arbitrary Power are in eternal enmity."

At first, the flaming invective of Burke during the trial, and the remarkable rhetorical performances of Fox and Sheridan, attracted eager crowds of spectators—the rank and fashion of England—to Westminster Hall; seats sold for as much as fifty guineas. But everyone grew weary as seven years elapsed; Burke himself found the trial a dread ordeal, perhaps suffering more than Hastings; yet he refrained for three years from retiring from the House of Commons (which he desperately wished to do, ridiculed and lampooned as he found himself in 1792) that he might carry on his denunciation of injustice to the bitter end. On May 28, 1794, he began to sum up before the Lords his work of sixteen years—in a speech which, lasting nine days, was a prolonged cry of passion and despair.

The rising generation, he burst out, might see the guilt of Hastings, and the fundamental truth that "merit cannot extinguish crime." His final appeal was to natural justice implanted in men's minds and hearts by Divine benevolence; on June 16, the last day of his agonizing effort—he retired from Parliament on June 20, 1794—he told the Lords that their own existence, and the survival of Britain, were bound up with justice in India:

> My Lords, it has pleased Providence to place us in such a state, that we appear every moment to be on the verge of some great mutations. There is one thing, and one thing only, which defies all mutation; that which existed before the world, and will survive the fabrick of the world itself; I mean justice; that justice, which, emanating from the Divinity, has a place in the breast of every one of us, given us for our guide with regard to ourselves, and with regard to others, and which will stand, after this globe is burned to ashes, our advocate or our accuser before the great Judge, when He comes to call upon us for the tenour of a well-spent life....

> My Lords, if you must fall, may you so fall! but if
> you stand, and stand I trust you will, together with
> the fortune of this ancient monarchy—together with
> the ancient laws and liberties of this great and illus-
> trious kingdom, may you stand as unimpeached in
> honour as in power; may you stand, not as a substi-
> tute for virtue, but as an ornament of virtue, as a
> security for virtue; may you stand long, and long
> stand the terrour of tyrants; may you stand the refuge
> of afflicted nations; may you stand a sacred temple,
> for the perpetual residence of an inviolable Justice.

On April 29, 1795, the House of Lords came to a verdict.
In the Tory government, Pitt and Dundas had believed
Hastings to be guilty of at least one or two of the sixteen
articles of the indictment. Loughborough, the Lord Chancellor, voted "guilty" on most of the charges. But the peers
found otherwise: by heavy majorities, they acquitted Warren Hastings on every count.

The mass of documents concerning the impeachment
and trial of Hastings is so overwhelming—not to mention
the endless labyrinth of the papers of the East India
Company, and other evidence never well sifted—that no
wholly satisfactory impartial analysis of Burke's charges
against Hastings has yet been made. The nearest approach
to this gigantic—and perhaps impossible—task, however,
is the accomplishment of Carl B. Cone, in the second
volume of his biography of Burke. His conclusions deserve
comment here.

It is Dr. Cone's considered judgment that Burke acted
on principle in his prosecution of Hastings, and not, except
incidentally, from partisan advantage or personal motives.

He opposed arbitrary government on principle; to legalize it for India was to repudiate the lessons of English history.... Burke hated tyranny in any form. The people of India as much as the English people deserved security against arbitrary power. Burke knew that his arguments had little appeal. But they demonstrated that his attack on Hastings...was directed against excessive concentration of power, which, if misused, meant abuse of the trust under which Britain held her imperial authority.

Philip Francis and William Burke, though they furnished their friend with information against Hastings, were only contributory to Burke's passionate prosecution of the master of India. Burke's assessment of Hastings' character was substantially accurate, Cone concludes, and the evidence of Hastings' wrong-doing was sufficient for indictment. Burke knew well enough that this cause could bring him only pain and trouble; it would drag him

through a nasty, mean, distressing business that exposed him to abuse, monopolized his time, required arduous labor, and promised no personal reward even if he achieved his purposes.

Nor was Burke turned by prejudice and partisanship from his early view that the East India Company should be free of government interference, to his later conviction that the British government must regulate the Company strictly, and deprive it of political authority. It was deeper acquaintance with Indian affairs, rather, which led Burke to his conclusion that "the chartered rights of men" ranked higher than the East India Company's charter. And practically, he found that a mercantile corporation was incompetent to perform the political function of administering justice.

Burke was justified in pressing the impeachment of Hastings, Cone argues. Although the Portland Whigs were a minority in the House of Commons, and although the power of Hastings and his friends was most formidable, the Governor-General was courageously and rightfully impeached:

> Burke thought it his duty to expose the nature of British administration in India in the hope that men might learn to act under the compulsion of morality as well as positive law.

In effect, Hastings' defense rested upon "necessities of state," even if Hastings himself did not take precisely that ground. Burke declared that the magistrate and the soldier may not be exempted by claims of a transient necessity from the law of nations or the canons of natural justice.

> Burke's impeachment of Hastings was one of his great causes. It does credit to his memory; it was a considerable part of his life; it was a major historical event. If his efforts ended in failure, he was not ashamed, nor had he any reason to be.

And yet, Cone continues, quite as the Commons were right in impeaching Hastings, so the Lords were right in acquitting him. In an interesting exercise, Cone asks his reader to put himself in the place of a judicious peer in Westminster Hall, 1795. Granted perfect objectivity, "If one reads the eleven volumes of the minutes of evidence and decides on that evidence alone, one must vote as the majority did, for the acquittal of Warren Hastings."

For though Hastings had violated the natural law and the "chartered rights of men" in India, he had not sufficiently offended against English statute and common law to warrant conviction.

> A sympathetic peer would commiserate with Burke in the impossibility of the task he had set for himself. While all men, informed by their consciences, admit the existence of right, they find it difficult not to soften the absoluteness of the concept by appeals to utility and expediency.... It does not denigrate Burke or his philosophy, nor does it weaken his sincerity, to say that he had no choice but to base his prosecution of Hastings on the doctrine of natural law.... The doctrine of reason of state had no superior as a purely secular argument. Burke had to appeal to a higher authority, and it could only be the spiritual, supernatural authority of divine law.[10]

Cone doubts whether Burke's denunciation of Hastings and his methods did much to improve British colonial and imperial policy during the nineteenth and twentieth centuries. True, this topic requires more painstaking study than it has received to the present. Yet one may suspect that Cone underestimates the subtle influence of Burke upon the mind of the educated Englishman. It was not necessary to employ the volumes of Burke on Indian affairs as a kind of crib, or to make Burke's sentiments formal guidelines for viceroys and secretaries of state for India. Rather, Burke's eloquence, taught in every grammar school and public school, impressed upon the boys who would become colonial officers and members of Parliament some part of Burke's sense of duty and consecration in the civil social order—with reference particularly to India and Empire.

An earlier perceptive biographer, Bertram Newman, remarks that as for India, Burke builded better than he knew; by his spectacular warning, he helped to bring justice to India thereafter.

> He was the first parliamentary statesman to devote the whole of his powers to the cause of India; the first to proclaim, and to inspire others to proclaim, that England had a duty to her subject peoples in the East; the first to express in words to which even apathy and hostility could not but listen, what has been highest in the motives that have since animated a long line of rulers.[11]

Burke believed his prosecuting of Hastings to be the best work of his life. In the final year of his life, he wrote to Dr. French Laurence (July 28, 1796) that Laurence must draw up a formal account and defense of the prosecution, since he himself was too far gone for that labor.

> Let not this cruel, daring, unexampled act of publick corruption, guilt, and meanness, go down to a posterity, perhaps as careless as the present race, without its due animadversion, which will be best found in its own acts and monuments. Let my endeavours to save the Nation from that shame and guilt, be my monument; The only one I ever will have. Let every thing I have done, said, or written, be forgotten, but this. I have struggled with the great and little on this point during the greater part of my

active life; and I wish after death, to have my defiance of the judgments of those, who consider the dominion of the glorious Empire given by an incomprehensible dispensation of the Divine Providence into our hands, as nothing more than an opportunity for gratifying, for the lowest of their purposes, the lowest of their passions—and that for such poor rewards, and for the most part, indirect and silly bribes, as indicate even more the folly than the corruption of these infamous and contemptible wretches.... Above all make out the cruelty of this pretended acquittal, but in reality this barbarous and inhuman condemnation of whole tribes and nations, and of all the classes they contain. If ever Europe recovers its civilization, that work will be useful. Remember! Remember! Remember![12]

In 1780, Burke had thought that nothing could be more important than the melancholy affairs of India—not even the plight of Ireland. But the Irish cauldron bubbled more menacingly during the years he spent upon the prosecution of Hastings; and while he was in the midst of Hastings' trial, Sansculotte started up in Paris, confronting Burke with matters of urgency greater even than justice in India. Revolution, the fourth horseman of the Apocalypse, had come dashing down upon the smug world of the eighteenth century, a king's head at his saddlebow.

6

The Verge of the Abyss

"The abyss of Hell itself seems to yawn before me," Burke was to write, in November, 1793, to Earl Fitzwilliam.[1] He referred to the political and moral revolution then being perpetrated by the triumphant Jacobins; but Jacobinism was only one agent of the destruction of the old order of things. Forty-seven years earlier, young Burke, at Trinity College, had prophesied to Shackleton, "We are just on the verge of Darkness and one push drives us in." Burke's vision had come to pass: revolution was clearing the way for the return of Saturn.

Burke's life was one long endeavor to avert or check revolution—in the American colonies, in the domestic order of Britain, in tormented India, in his native Ireland, in France and the whole of the European continent. While Burke sat, seemingly secure, with Johnson and Reynolds and Goldsmith and the rest in their Club, the old order was passing. Burke heard the dread echoes of "The World Turned Upside Down" at Yorktown and, presently, of the "Carmagnole" at Paris.

Few besides Burke ventured to predict that the cozy
world of the eighteenth century would be terminated by
the return of the gods of the copybook headings. Proud of
its rationality and its progress, the age took for granted its
own virtual perfection and its own virtual immortality.
Writing, at the end of the Directory, a fiction founded on
his own recollections, the critic and dramatist La Harpe
describes the climate of opinion which had prevailed
among people of Burke's station, in France as in Britain,
just before the catastrophic events of 1789.

La Harpe imagines a dinner at the house of a member of
the French Academy, the company most fashionable, "of
every profession, courtiers, advocates, men of letters and
Academicians." Their talk is uninhibited and sanguine:

> One of the guests narrates, bursting with laughter,
> what a hairdresser said to him while powdering his
> hair: 'You see, sir, although I am a miserable scrub,
> I have no more religion than any one else.' They
> conclude that the Revolution soon will be consum-
> mated, that superstition and fanaticism must give
> way wholly to philosophy, and they thus calculate
> the probabilities of the epoch and those of the future
> society which will see the reign of reason. The most
> aged lament not being able to flatter themselves that
> they will see it; the young rejoice in a reasonable
> prospect of seeing it, and especially do they congratu-
> late the Academy on having paved the way for the
> great work and in having been the headquarters, the
> centre, the inspirer of freedom of thought.

Yet one of the guests, Jacques Cazotte, something of a
mystic, dissents from this rosy consensus. He predicts to

the scandalized ears of his host and fellow guests that within six years nearly everyone present will perish by violence, in agony and terror. They hope Cazotte jests:

> 'But then we shall have been overcome by Turks or Tartars?' 'By no means; you will be governed as I have already told you, solely by philosophy and reason. Those who are to treat you in this manner will all be philosophers, will all, at every moment, have on their lips the phrases you have uttered within the hour, will repeat your maxims, will quote, like yourselves, the stanzas of Diderot and of "La Pucelle."'

If this is a jest, its taste is questionable—though in this charming circle, every freedom of speech had been indulged.

> 'Well, these are miracles,' exclaims La Harpe, 'and you leave me out?'—'You will be no less a miracle, for you will then be a Christian.'—'Ah,' interposes Champfort, 'I breathe again; if we are to die only when La Harpe becomes a Christian, we are immortals.'

Cazotte, nevertheless, continues to prophesy. Women—princesses of the blood, and greater than these—will not be spared: they will go to the scaffold with their hands tied behind their backs. Madame de Gramont, despite her frivolous plea to Cazotte, will not be allowed a confessor, for

> 'the last of the condemned that will have one, as an act of grace, will be....' He stopped a moment. 'Tell me, now, who is the fortunate mortal enjoying this pre-

rogative?'—'It is the last that will remain to him, and it will be the King of France.'[2]

Like the seer of the *Prophétie de Cazotte,* Edmund Burke possessed vaticinatory powers. That Sansculotte never started up in England was in part the work of Burke the reformer and Burke the inspired foe of the "armed doctrine." The fourth horseman of the Apocalypse[3] never rode frantic into Westminster—though, at his dying day, Edmund Burke feared all was lost. But most of the civilized world, between 1775 and 1815, endured revolutionary agony until Napoleon said of himself, "I have laid the fell spectre of Innovation which was bestriding all the universe." (Indeed, the world suffered the consequences of radical alteration for some years after Bonaparte spoke.)

Burke foresaw the American Revolution, and was unable to prevent its coming; he predicted that Ireland would go the way of America, if reforms were not undertaken promptly—and so Ireland did; he prophesied that the French Revolution would rend Europe limb from limb until subdued by force and a master—and that, too, came to pass. The smug optimism of the Enlightenment did not infect him. In this chapter, we are concerned with Burke's dread of an anarchic upheaval, fearfully vindicated by the violence which commenced in 1789. The revolution of humanitarian rationalism, so eagerly anticipated by La Harpe and his friends, a few months earlier, did not occur: a very different kind of revolution pushed them over the verge of darkness.

In Burke's native Ireland, revolution approached during the last months of his life, and continued sporadically for a century and a quarter. Though the whole intricate story of Burke's part in Irish concerns cannot be related here, it is possible to outline the course which Burke followed in the hope of preventing rebellion and ultimate secession from the British Empire. Participation in Irish affairs ran all through Burke's political life, but coincided especially with his prosecuting of Hastings and with his countermining of the French Revolution. At the last, after retiring from the Commons, Burke spent even more time upon Irish matters than he did upon the European revolution. Burke's Irish labors suggest his general alternative to revolutionary destruction and the "armed doctrine."

Burke saw the whole of the nation with "the fancy of a poet, and dwelt on it with the eye of a lover," Augustine Birrell says.

> But love is the parent of fear, and none knew better than Burke how thin is the lava layer between the costly fabric of society and the volcanic heats and destroying flames of anarchy. He trembled for the fair fame of all established things, and to his horror saw men, instead of covering the thin surface with the concrete, digging in it for abstractions, and asking fundamental questions about the origin of society, and why one man should be born rich and another poor.... Burke, as he regarded humanity swarming like bees into and out of their hives of industry, is ever asking himself, How are these men to be saved from anarchy?[4]

So Burke set his face against all revolutions, which have a way of devouring their children. The American Revolution he looked upon as a dreary calamity, produced by madness and vanity on either side of the Atlantic. After the peace made in 1782, however, he hoped that the United States might prosper: theirs, after all, had not been a real revolution so much as it had been a war of independence. Though he feared the rise of democracy in the Southern states, he much admired the Federalists, Washington in particular. Like the "Glorious Revolution," America's upheaval might be not so much a revolution made, as one prevented. If the Americans sought by political means to establish an unnatural equality of condition, they would work immense mischief upon themselves.

"You know that it is this very rage for equality, which has blown up the Flames of this present cursed War in America," he had written to John Bourke, in 1777.[5] But the American respect for law (as he had declared during his effort at conciliation, the Americans were mightily read in Blackstone's *Commentaries*) and for constitution might yet give them ordered freedom.

Burke anticipated Alexis de Tocqueville—whom his writings strongly influenced—in wishing that that "new State of a new Species in a new part of the Globe" might reconcile innovation with permanence. As Ross Hoffman points out,

> Every basic value Burke cherished—liberty with order, right morals, justice, and social freedom from arbitrary power—Tocqueville hoped that the new democratic society, which in spite of his misgivings he welcomed, would somehow retain or revive.[6]

As democracy was suspect to the Federalists, so was that

scheme of government alien to Burke. He stood always in opposition to arbitrary power—the will of the monarch, unchecked, or the will of the mob, unhedged. In Burke's first parliamentary years, the Rockinghams had learnt what untrustworthy allies were the "patriot" enthusiasts for John Wilkes. (It was Wilkes' radical supporters of the Society for the Bill of Rights who most ferociously fulminated against the doctrines of Burke's *Present Discontents.*) However temporarily useful to the Rockinghams the cause of the rascally Wilkes might be, Burke knew the licentious demagogue's partisans for his actual or potential enemies. As Burke wrote to Shackleton, the leveling democrats at Wilkes' back were

> a rotten subdivision of a Faction amongst us, who have done us infinite mischief by the violence, rashness, and often wickedness of their measures, I mean the Bill of rights people but who have thought proper at length to do us I hope a service, by declaring open war upon all our connection.[7]

Yet there were rougher folk than the demonstrators for Wilkes in the Middlesex Elections. The eighteenth-century London mob was quite as merciless, potentially, as the sanguinary rabble that was to follow the tumbrils of Paris, to see women bare their necks "white as chickens' flesh" (as a concierge, well after the Terror, told Chateaubriand, gloatingly). How a handful of fanatics might rouse the population of the slums to destroy all order, Burke learnt by experience in 1780: the Gordon Riots illustrated his principle that the savage lies just under the skin of many a man.

In 1778, Catholic Relief Acts, nominally sponsored by Sir George Savile and Lord Richard Cavendish, but actually drawn up by Burke, much modified in both England and Ireland the penal laws against Catholics. But at the mere suggestion of a similar relief for Scottish Catholics, the zealots of the Kirk rose up in tumultuous wrath, attacking Catholic chapels and communicants in the Scottish burghs. The terrified Scottish Catholics presently sent to Burke a petition for protection and relief; Burke presented the petition to the House of Commons on March 18, 1779. The Commons took no action on the petition that session, but the introduction of the plea was sufficient to send into a raving fit the eccentric (and nearly lunatic) Lord George Gordon—then the most enthusiastic of "No Popery" Protestants, later to profess Judaism. Gordon appealed to the ignorant London crowd, always mindful of "Remember, remember, the fifth of November, Guy Fawkes and the Gunpowder Plot." On June 2, 1780, Gordon tramped up to Westminster with the petition of the Protestant Association of England, asking Parliament to repeal the Catholic Relief Act. Sixty-thousand ruffians from the Warrens of London were at his back. In *Barnaby Rudge*, Charles Dickens describes the fashion in which this pious gathering endeavored to persuade Lords and Commons to do the alleged will of the people. This was the day upon which that repellent apprentice Simon Tappertit, coming home from the scenes at Westminster, startled his master's household:

> 'This,' he added, putting his hand into his waistcoat pocket, and taking out a large tooth, at the sight of which both Miggs and Mrs. Varden screamed, 'this was a bishop's. Beware, G. Varden!'

The Archbishop of York, indeed, had been beaten by the mob, as he tried to enter Westminster Hall, and the Bishop of Lincoln had fled over housetops. Dickens draws a true picture of the conduct of the loyal followers of Lord George Gordon at the doors of the Mother of Parliaments:

> Through this vast throng, sprinkled doubtless here and there with honest zealots, but composed for the most part of the very scum and refuse of London, whose growth was fostered by bad criminal laws, bad prison regulations, and the worst conceivable police, such of the members of both Houses of Parliament as had not taken the precaution to be already at their posts, were compelled to fight and force their way. Their carriages were stopped and broken; the wheels wrenched off; drivers, footmen, and Masters, pulled from their seats and rolled in the mud. Lords, commoners, and reverend bishops, with little distinction of person or party, were kicked and pinched and hustled; passed from hand to hand through various stages of ill-usage; and sent to their fellow-senators at last with their clothes hanging in ribbons about them, their bagwigs torn off, covered with the powder which had been cuffed and beaten out of their hair. One lord was so long in the hands of the populace, that the Peers as a body resolved to sally forth and rescue him, and were in the act of doing so, when he happily reappeared among them covered with dirt and bruises, and hardly to be recognized by those who knew him best. The noise and uproar were on the increase every moment. The air was filled with execrations, hoots, and howlings. The mob raged and roared like a mad monster as it was, unceasingly, and each new outrage served to swell its fury.

So commenced the Gordon Riots, which continued for days, the mob breaking into and burning down the jails, destroying the Catholic chapels, sacking and setting fire to the houses of Lord Mansfield and scores of others, storming the Bank of England, and threatening to murder all friends of toleration for Papists. Some four hundred and fifty people died—chiefly in the street—fighting with the military. Burke, in peril because he was rightly suspected of being the real sponsor of the Relief Acts, behaved with high courage in the streets and in Parliament. The mob shouted that he was a Jesuit in disguise, and once he drew his sword to defend himself. When the troops had put down the insurrection, Burke wrote to the Lord Chancellor to ask for mercy toward most of the captured rioters.[8]

This occurred nine years before the Parisian mob stormed the Bastille. Had Burke required any more reason to doubt the alleged abstract virtue of an abstract "People," postulated by the *philosophes,* the Gordon Riots would have supplied his evidence. Amid the smoke of half-ruined London, he knew that the anonymous and faceless tyranny of the revolutionary mob was a worse thing than even the most unfeeling despotism.

Knowing Ireland better, perhaps, than any other man eminent in the House of Commons, Burke understood that worse than the Gordon Riots might come to pass in John Bull's Other Island, were not political and economic reform undertaken soon. This concern for Irish Catholics and Irish commerce cost him his Bristol seat; but, undeterred, after 1780 he labored even harder than before on behalf of Irish welfare; and for some years, he was successful.

Burke was sincerely an Anglican; he remarked once that, having read all the tracts of the preceding age on the claims of Catholicism and Protestantism, he found himself more bewildered than when he began, and so settled for the Church of England by law established. His religious convictions were very like those of the judicious Richard Hooker, sentences from whose *Laws of Ecclesiastical Polity* were quoted or paraphrased now and again in Burke's speeches, books, and conversation.

Yet the oppressed Catholics—more than two-thirds of the whole population of Ireland—had no warmer friend. Had the "No Popery" folk known how Catholic was Burke's background, they would have been even more incensed against him. Not only were his mother and his sister Catholics, but his father, Richard Burke, was the lawyer of James Cotter, Jr., an Irish Catholic leader who was hanged for rape (a judicial lynching) in 1720. The elder Burke himself had been a Catholic, but recanted and conformed to the Church of Ireland in 1722, perhaps to relieve his family from the burden of the Penal Laws. On the distaff side, the Nagle family (Burke's mother's people) were not only Catholic, but Jacobite: Sir Richard Nagle was minister of war, in Ireland, to James II, and followed his master into exile; Garrett Nagle of Ballygriffin was accused, in 1731, of being a chief agent for the exiled Pretender.[9] Thus Edmund Burke had reasons of family, as well as of prudence, for opposing the Protestant Ascendency in Ireland.

That country might be saved from rebellion, Burke held,

by three principal measures: relief and emancipation of Catholics, freeing of Irish commerce, and reduction of the Ascendency. He would have given Ireland effective political autonomy (free even of the legislative superiority of the English Parliament, which is more than he conceded to America), under the Crown; would have allowed Catholics to sit in the Irish Parliament and to hold military and civil offices; would have extended the franchise to the more responsible among them; and would have obtained free trade for Irish manufactures.

Only thus might the principal Irish grievances be remedied; half measures would not suffice; the reform, though to be accomplished gradually in some of its details, should commence at once, before loyalty diminished and tempers rose.

His closest Irish ally was Henry Grattan, leader of the opposition in the Irish Parliament—like Burke, an Anglican, but also bent on bringing down the narrow clique of the Ascendency. It was the work of these two, chiefly, that effected much improvement of Irish affairs between 1780 and 1795; yet in the end they were unable to carry the British government and the dominant Protestant minority in Ireland far enough to retain Ireland as a contented partner in the imperial structure.

The fragmentary concessions grudgingly made by British Crown and Parliament to the Irish were the result of a gnawing dread—alarm first at the menace of the Americans, and then at the menace of the French. Should the Irish join with these enemies, Britain would be in wretched plight. Burke and others, intent on preserving the Empire—but an Empire with justice—were able to take some advantage of this London disquietude to ameliorate the lot of Ireland.

From the raising of the Irish Volunteers, in 1778, came the first strong pressure. This was a militia quite unauthorized by the government, raised to protect Ireland from the threat of American or French naval incursions—or even landings in force—during the American Revolution. The Volunteers were altogether Protestant, initially, though Catholics were admitted later; by the summer of 1779, there were thirty thousand of them, commanded by Lord Charlemont.[10] They could defend Ireland against foreign enemies—or, as Burke feared, they might be used to resist British authority. The existence of these troops helped to induce North's ministry to adopt the Catholic Relief Act of 1788 and to open colonial markets to Irish merchants two years later. Irish Dissenters were relieved from the Test Act in 1780, so that members of the Church of Ireland no longer wholly monopolized public offices and the franchise: only Catholics still were excluded. In 1782 the Rockingham ministry made the Irish Parliament independent of the British Parliament—though this was a nominal Irish autonomy, for the most part, since the Crown, through the apparatus of Dublin Castle and the Ascendency, still controlled the Irish Parliament that met in its splendid classical hall (now the Bank of Ireland) beside College Green. Burke was most active in all these reforms; but he knew that more were required.

Although the severity of the Penal Laws had been diminished, and although the remaining code was not always strictly enforced, Irish Catholics continued to suffer from gross exclusions. They were forbidden to enter the legal profession, to teach medicine, to study in the university, to hold civil or military offices, to serve on grand juries, or to vote. They had no representation, actual or virtual, in the Irish Parliament. And yet they were at least two-thirds of the population.

Burke always had denied—from close knowledge—that the Irish Catholics were disloyal to Crown and Parliament, or that they had intrigued with foreign powers, or that they meant to make the Pope master of Ireland, or that they were disproportionately numerous in civil disturbances. It was not their religion which made Irish Catholics restive, he said, but their lack of potatoes.

With the outbreak of the French Revolution, nevertheless, it seemed all too possible that the Catholic majority might be tempted to waver in their loyalty. The original threat came not from them (for the Catholics still were dominated by the small band of Catholic country gentlemen and by the growing class of substantial merchants, never squinting toward Jacobinism), but from the Society of United Irishmen, founded in 1791, with Wolfe Tone at their head. These were radical Presbyterians, chiefly Ulstermen, fervent nationalists who would fight, if need be (indeed, would fight by preference, were there any remote possibility of success), to emulate America in obtaining total independence, and to emulate revolutionary France in establishing a nationalistic democracy.

The United Irishmen invited the Catholics to join forces with them. Should such a union be accomplished, Britain might have a deadly enemy at her back, while straining every nerve in the struggle with Jacobin France.

Burke had not been on Irish soil since 1786; indeed, he

never again would find leisure to visit Dublin or the Nagle Country. What Burke could do for the Empire and for Ireland, in this hour, was to write, and to act in Parliament—and to send his son.

Richard Burke, Edmund's only child, did not inherit his father's genius; few sons of great men do. Disliked by some who met him, he retained a high opinion of his own talents, nevertheless. Through him, the great father—who loved his son with all his passionate heart—hoped to found a noble house, taking a peerage on his retirement from the Commons. But somehow this handsome young man had obtained no footing in life. With some misgiving, but thankful that any opportunity for Richard to grow in influence should appear, Edmund Burke assented when Father Hussey, the most intelligent of the Irish Catholic leaders, invited Richard to become agent for the Irish Catholic Committee, the political arm of the oppressed Irish majority. At the end of December, 1791, Richard arrived in Dublin to take up his duties, which involved close attendance upon the sittings of the Irish Parliament.

At the same time, Edmund Burke completed his pamphlet, in the form of a letter to Sir Hercules Langrishe, on the Irish Catholics. It was intended as a manual for Richard, as a commentary on Langrishe's intended bill for further Catholic relief, and as a program for action by Parliament. This *Letter to Sir Hercules Langrishe...on the Subject of the Roman Catholics of Ireland and the Propriety of Admitting Them to the Elective Franchise* is Burke's chief analysis of the Irish problem.

Burke's principal point was that a commonwealth dare not exclude from active participation in its affairs and privileges a great mass of its population. "A plebeian oligarchy is a monster"; and since the Irish government was not wholly aristocratic, it tended toward an oligarchy of Protestant plebeians which ruled the majority of Irishmen against their will. "The Protestants of Ireland are not *alone* sufficiently the people to form a democracy; and they are *too numerous* to answer the ends and purposes of *an aristocracy.*"

Burke detested the Protestant Ascendency not because it was Protestant, not because it kept power in the hands of a comparative few, but rather because it made no provision at all for representing the overwhelming majority of Irishmen—nay, it kept them down mercilessly. The Ascendency was destroying Irishmen's loyalty to Britain. The unreformed Parliament and the limited franchise of England and Scotland were not unjust, because the large majority of the British people were represented virtually, if not "actually" (that is, in any regular system of representation founded on a mathematical formula), by a Parliament that was concerned for the general good. There was no gulf fixed between the custodians of power and the English people. But in Ireland, the Irish Parliament, dominated by the Ascendency, represented only one-third of the nation, and yet presumed to treat the Irish majority as if Catholics somehow stood outside the state.

> Are we to be astonished, when, by the efforts of so much violence in conquest, and so much policy in regulation, continued without intermission for near a hundred years, we had reduced them to a mob, without temper, measure, or foresight? ...If the disorder you speak of be real and considerable, you

ought to raise an aristocratic interest—that is, an
interest of property and education—amongst them,
and to strengthen, by every prudent means, the authority and influence of men of that description.

Burke would admit the Catholics to a share in the constitution, chiefly by letting them vote on the same terms as
those enjoyed by Protestants, or at least by allowing them
some genuine representation:

> Our constitution is not made for great, general, or
> prescriptive exclusions; sooner or later it will destroy
> them, or they will destroy the constitution. In our
> constitution there has always been a difference be-
> tween *a franchise* and *an office*, and between the cap-
> acity for one and for the other. Franchises were sup-
> posed to belong to the *subject*, as a *subject*, and not as
> a member of the governing part of the state. The gov-
> ernment has considered them as things different;
> for, whilst Parliament excluded by the test acts (and
> for a while these test acts were not a dead letter, as now
> they are in England) Protestant Dissenters from all
> civil and military employments, they *never touched
> their right of voting for members of Parliament or sitting
> in either house;* a point I state, not as approving or
> condemning, with regards to them, the measure of
> exclusion from employments, but to prove that the
> distinction has become admitted in legislature, as, in
> truth, it is founded in nature.[11]

The Irish Dissenters—the United Irishmen—said Burke,
offer the Catholics complete equality. Should not the
government act to satisfy Catholics, before such an incongruous alliance be consummated? The Catholic and French-

speaking inhabitants of Canada had remained loyal to the Crown when the English-speaking colonies had risen in revolt. Should not the ministry, by dealing generously with the Irish Catholics, persuade these subjects to a similar fealty?

By late February, Pitt's ministry and Parliament—together with the Irish Parliament, whose decision nominally settled the whole question—made minor concessions. Langrishe's bill for Catholic Relief was adopted—though the Burkes looked upon it as "not only no relief, but...mischievous and insolent." It permitted Catholics to practice law, to marry Protestants, to open schools without consent of the Church of Ireland establishment, and to send their children abroad to be educated. These small favors, reluctantly yielded, did not diminish Catholic agitation; and because Richard Burke had not succeeded in obtaining more than half a loaf, the Catholic Committee relieved him of his Dublin duties—giving him a plump purse by way of recompense—though retaining him as their London agent.

In 1793, the government made grander concessions; for the pressure from the Burkes was succeeding; and in the year of the Terror, the Irish Catholics must not be allowed to drift into the arms of the subversive United Irishmen. The new act enabled Catholics to vote on the same terms as Protestants, although still they could not sit in Parliament or hold any really important office. (They were now permitted to become magistrates, however, to serve on grand juries, to obtain military commissions, and to take university degrees.)

By this relief of 1793, nevertheless, the Catholic gentry

and upper-middle classes gained next to nothing: the poor and ignorant were enfranchised, Burke complained mordantly, but the leading Catholics could not enter Parliament or occupy important offices—though no one needed aristocratic leadership more urgently than did the Catholic Irish. Yet Burke did not desire to have the electorate composed merely of the affluent: a year earlier, he had been vexed at a proposal within the Catholic Committee to enfranchise every Catholic possessing property that produced an income of a hundred pounds a year, but none poorer. This, he had said, was oligarchy all over again.

So the Ascendency still held power, exacerbating Catholic tempers, notwithstanding the extension of the franchise. So long as the Parliament House and Dublin Castle were monopolized by the arrogant and unimaginative few families of the Ascendency, Burke knew, some of the Irish would flirt with revolution.

Burke, Grattan, and their allies had gained much ground in a few years—yet not enough to placate the Catholics, let alone the leveling United Irishmen. Only the opening of Parliament and of the chief offices of government to Catholics could have secured the fealty of the majority of the Irish population; but this was not to be.

The final defeat of Burke's plan for conciliation of the Irish was the failure of his friend Earl Fitzwilliam—successor of Lord Rockingham—to achieve the crowning reform on which both of them had pinned their hopes. Early in January, 1795, Fitzwilliam arrived in Dublin as Lord Lieutenant, sent by the coalition ministry of Portland and Pitt. He endeavored boldly to obtain prompt Catholic "emancipation"—that is, an act enabling Catholics to stand for the

Irish Parliament and to occupy state offices of trust. But Fitzwilliam alienated powerful families of the Ascendency; also his design shocked the King, whose stubborn heart was resolved on giving nothing more to Catholics, lest he violate the oath he had taken at his coronation to uphold the Anglican establishment; and Pitt, having other Irish schemes in view, did not support Fitzwilliam. Before two months were out, Fitzwilliam was recalled to London. As Hoffman and Levack comment,

> The Protestant ascendency was maintained and Catholic flirtation with the United Irishmen increased. Currents were released which flowed on the one hand toward the revolutionary rising of 1798, and on the other toward the extinction of the Irish kingdom through organic union with Britain in 1800.[12]

Meanwhile, Wolfe Tone, admirer of Danton and Tom Paine, hard hater of the Burkes, had succeeded Richard Burke as agent for the Catholic Committee. He was a man of violence, and in religion far more distant from his Catholic principals than were the Burkes. Entering into negotiations with the French, he proceeded to plot revolution; and after vicissitudes (including a sojourn in America, which he disliked, calling George Washington "a high-flying aristocrat") he made his way toward his doom. In 1798, as adjutant-general of a French force attempting the invasion of Ireland, he was taken in a naval fight; sentenced to death, he cut his throat. A century and a quarter of Irish revolution had commenced, with the fanatic Tone as martyr-in-chief.

Edmund Burke never knew of Wolfe Tone's rising; for he had died sixteen months earlier, having done his best for Ireland and for Empire.

"Possessed of a mind which instinctively loved and fully appreciated truth," Thomas Mahoney writes of Burke,

> he felt strongly both the injustice and inexpediency of the treatment accorded the Irish Catholics. He bitterly condemned their proscription as the wretched invention of a lust for power by those who stood to profit by keeping the Catholics weak. To correct these abuses he relied in large measure upon a policy of expediency, which was by no means opportunism. To him expedience meant that which was good for the entire community, collectively and individually. To realize the expedient required diligent search through the long slow process of social organization. There one could find those principles of both civil and religious freedom whereby the good of the Irish community could be achieved.... Had he been heeded and the blueprint which he had drawn up for the solution of Ireland's problems, particularly those of the Catholics, been followed, it seems patent that Ireland's long and dreary history in the nineteenth and much of the twentieth centuries need not have occurred.[13]

Late in October, 1786, on his last visit to Ireland, somehow Burke found time to return for a day to Ballitore, where he had learnt so much from Abraham Shackleton. Now his preceptor's grandson was master in the school. The statesman missed trees that had been cut down since his time, and remembered well those that still stood; he sought out all his old friends, in his genial, open way, and

was much gaped at. Ireland would not look upon his like
again, nor he upon Ireland.

By 1798, Wolfe Tone's Wicklow rebels were fighting the
troops at Ballitore; everything was destroyed. In Kildare, as
in France, the abyss had opened. But Edmund Burke lay in
his secret grave at Beaconsfield, all passion spent.

7

A Revolution
of Theoretic Dogma

Burke's greatest hour came to him late. When the Paris mob stormed the Bastille, slaughtered its garrison of pensioners, and scattered its stones abroad, Edmund Burke was sixty years old: a party leader who had been out of office most of his career, an orator celebrated for his championing the cause of the unfortunate—but also, in 1789, a man whose reputation had declined. His immoderate zeal in the "Regency crisis" at the time of George III's first fit of madness had damaged his fair fame;[1] and then the King had recovered, to make Burke a laughingstock. He was unpopular with many, too, because of his prosecution of Hastings and his solicitude for Irish Catholics.

Already he thought of retirement from Parliament. Within his party, the suppler Fox had surpassed him in power—and, many said, in eloquence; after Rockingham's death, Burke's influence among the grand Whigs had diminished. Even to himself, he seemed to contend against the stars in their courses: Hastings, he knew, would go free; the Tories were well entrenched in office; his own affairs proceeded badly. He struggled for Catholic emancipation; should he not soon ask for the Chiltern Hundreds, seeking his own emancipation from "crooked politicks?"

Then, of a sudden, Sansculottism asked, "What think ye of me?" Burke's prompt reply was his most enduring gift to the rising generation and to those yet unborn.

> Burke gave the most striking proofs of his charac-
> ter and genius in the evil days in which his life ended—
> not when he was a leader in the Commons, but when
> he was a stricken old man at Beaconsfield.

So wrote Woodrow Wilson.

> What a man was you may often discover in the
> records of his days of bitterness and pain better than
> in what is told of his seasons of cheer and hope; for if
> the noble qualities triumph then and show them-
> selves still sound and sweet, if his courage sink not, if
> he show himself still capable of self-forgetfulness, if he
> still stir with a passion for the service of causes and
> polities which are beyond himself, his stricken age is
> even greater than his full-pulsed years of manhood.
> This is the test which Burke endures—the test of fire.[2]

Edmund Burke never had feared to attack the powerful, or to defend the weak, or to oppose to established interests the high power of his imagination. His chief constructive measure had been the Economical Reform, which mightily amended the structure and operation of the Civil List, in despite of everything that placeholders and royal influence could do to prevent him. He had been the most outspoken champion of oppressed Catholics—and, often, of Dissenters. He had insisted, when first he rose to eminence in the

House of Commons, that Americans possessed both the rights of Englishmen and the prescriptive usages which they had acquired in the course of their colonial experience. He had steadfastly opposed all policies calculated to reduce private liberties, to centralize authority in the Crown, or to diminish the prerogatives of Parliament. His generous sympathies for the chartered rights of civilized men extended far beyond England and Ireland, to Quebec and Madras. Even his own party—let alone the Crown—never had rewarded him properly for his courage, his brilliance, his scholarship, and his energy. It seemed, therefore, to many of the leaders of liberal opinion in revolutionary France (which country Burke had visited thrice, returning to London dismayed at the rise of atheism among the French) that Burke, more than any other English political leader, was admirably calculated to head in Britain a radical movement of reform on French principles.

But the French radicals reckoned without their man. At one time or another, Mirabeau, Thomas Paine, "Anacharsis" Cloots, and a young gentleman named DePont had visited Burke at Beaconsfield, and had enjoyed his kindnesses; the latter three wrote to him, in 1789, in the expectation that he would approve their sweeping alteration of French institutions.[3] They had mistaken Burke's whole nature. He was not a man of the Enlightenment, but a Christian, much read in Aristotle, Cicero, the Fathers of the Church, the Schoolmen (including Aquinas) and the great English divines. The presumption of the Age of Reason roused Burke's indignation and contempt. Endowed with a prophet's vision, he marvelously foresaw the whole course of events which would follow upon the French attempt to reconstruct society after an abstract pattern. The Revolution, after careering fiercely through a series of stages of hysterical violence, would end in a despotism; but by that time, it would have brought down in ruins most of what was fine and noble in traditional society. Burke resolved that Britain should not share in France's folly, and that the whole of the civilized world must be awakened to the menace of these abstractions of impractical speculators, which would expose mankind to the cruelty of the brute that lurks beneath our fallen human nature, instead of conjuring up the Noble Savage of romantic fiction.

As Lord Percy of Newcastle writes, Burke was the chief formulator of the modern Christian understanding of true civil freedom: yet he has been

> until quite recently, almost persistently misunderstood. His party pamphlets have been taken as sound history, while his anti-revolutionary philosophy has been dismissed as a crotchet of old age and declining powers. This is almost the exact reverse of the truth. Burke was a Whig partisan, no more reliable as a witness to contemporary fact than any other party politician. But, as other such politicians have not seldom been shocked into statesmanship by war, he was shocked into philosophy by, first, the American and, then, the French Revolution.[4]

Much read in history and much practiced in the conduct of political affairs, Burke knew that men are not naturally good, but are beings of mingled good and evil, kept in obedience to a moral law chiefly by the force of custom and habit, which the revolutionaries would discard as so much antiquated rubbish. He knew that all the advantages of society are the product of intricate human experience over many centuries, not to be amended overnight by some coffee-house philosopher. He knew religion to be man's greatest good, and established order to be the principal necessity of civilization, and hereditary possessions to be the prop of liberty and justice, and the mass of beliefs we often call "prejudices" to be the moral sense of humanity. He set his face against the revolutionaries like a man who finds himself suddenly beset by robbers.

Burke had defended the claims of some of the American colonists because they were the "chartered rights of Englishmen" overseas, developed by an historical process. He attacked the fallacy of the "Rights of Man," expounded by the French theorists, because he recognized in this abstract notion of rights an insensate desire to be emancipated from all duties. Unlike the "Glorious Revolution" of 1688, the French Revolution was intended to uproot the delicate growth that is human society; if not impeded, this revolutionary passion would end by subjecting all men first to anarchy and then to a ruthless master. In the pursuit of pretended abstract rights, men would have lost all real prescriptive rights.

Burke's reaction was then, and later, astounding to the votaries of the cult of Progress. In the middle of the nineteenth century, the historian Buckle argued that Burke must have gone mad in 1789. But men of the twentieth century have had much experience of revolutions undertaken on unexamined *a priori* assumptions; so few echo Buckle's theory today. The madness was rather that of the *philosophes* and people of fashion to whom Cazotte uttered his bloody prophecies: theirs was what Edmund Burke called "metaphysical madness," a rationalistic lunacy, founded upon a fantastic misunderstanding of human nature.[4] In Woodrow Wilson's phrase, "Burke was right, and was himself, when he sought to keep the French infection out of England."[6]

In Parliament, Burke's majestic denunciations of the Revolution at first had little effect. His own close friend and fellow leader of the Whigs, Charles James Fox, looked upon the French upheaval as a splendid triumph of progress and liberty; while William Pitt, though more cautious, thought the collapse of the French monarchy's authority more an opportunity for English advantage in the old rivalry than a menace to established English society. Perceiving that he must appeal beyond St. Stephen's Chapel to the sound sense of the British public, Burke set to work writing a tremendous pamphlet, which became the most brilliant work of English political philosophy, and which for eloquence combined with wisdom has no equal in any language's literature of politics: *Reflections on the Revolution in France,* published on November 1, 1790. This began as a letter to a young French friend, Charles DePont, who had visited Burke at Gregories in 1785 and had commenced a correspondence with him in the first stages of the Revolution, asking for Burke's opinion whether the French would succeed (knowing how to distinguish between liberty and license) in creating a better order.

DePont doubtless expected a favorable reply. But Burke, suspicious of certain tendencies of the Revolution from the first, within a few months perceived that the revolutionaries actually were subverting true "social freedom," which is maintained by wise laws and well-constructed institutions; they were seeking what never can be found, perfect liberty—which must mean that the bonds of social community are dissolved, and men are left little human atoms, at war with one another. By November, 1789, Burke was thoroughly alarmed—especially by a sermon of the radical Unitarian minister Dr. Richard Price, a friend of Lord Shelburne. Price had talked of "cashiering kings." Thus the purported letter to DePont actually commenced as a denunciation of Price's errors, and then developed into a defense of tradition, prescription, and the established order of civilized society against the radical innovators.

This book can no more be analyzed competently here than one could condense the writings of Plato, say, into a few paragraphs: the *Reflections* must be read by anyone who wishes to understand the great controversies of modern politics.[7] In this chapter, it is possible only to suggest Burke's principal arguments and overwhelming eloquence.

The immediate effect of the *Reflections* was powerful. Burke's popularity had been at its lowest ebb, especially after the partisan contest concerned with the state of the Crown during the temporary madness of George III; Fox, Burke, and other Portland Whigs had harmed themselves by their support of the Prince of Wales' claim to a regency by right. What Burke never expected, his tract abruptly raised him high in the opinion of the strong majority of the literate public. The King himself (his wits recovered) said that the *Reflections* was "a good book, a very good book; and every gentleman ought to read it." Nearly every gentleman did.

Most of the Tories, some of the Portland Whigs, and a great many people who ordinarily took little active part in

English politics, began to perceive the dread danger of revolution, and shifted toward that course of action which, in the long run, would crush Napoleon. Fox's Whigs, on the contrary, cried down Burke as an apostate, and in time the Duke of Bedford was rash enough to accuse Burke of self-seeking—which, after Burke's retirement from the House of Commons, provoked Burke's crushing reply, *A Letter to a Noble Lord.* A flood of pamphlets in answer to Burke's book appeared; in English, the two most influential retorts were those of James Mackintosh and Thomas Paine.[8] As the Revolution progressed, Mackintosh confessed that Burke was altogether right, becoming one of Burke's ablest disciples; and though Paine never disavowed his own radicalism, his narrow escape from the guillotine in Paris was some refutation of his early high hopes for liberty, equality, and fraternity.

Burke, said Paine, pitied the plumage but forgot the dying bird:

> When we see a man dramatically lamenting in a publication intended to be believed that '*The Age of chivalry is gone!* that *The glory of Europe is extinguished for ever!* that *The unbought grace of life* (if anyone knows what it *is*), *the cheap defense of nations, the nurse of manly sentiment and heroic enterprise is gone!*' and all this because the Quixot age of chivalry nonsense is gone, what opinion can we form of his judgment, or what regard can we pay to his facts? In the rhapsody of his imagination he has discovered a world of wind mills, and his sorrows are that there are no Quixots to attack them. But if the age of aristocracy, like that of chivalry, should fall (and they had originally some connection), Mr. Burke, the trum-

peter of the order, may continue his parody to the
end, and finish with exclaiming: '*Othello's occupation's
gone!*'

This passage is from *The Rights of Man.* In the minds of
liberals as well as the minds of conservatives, however,
from Woodrow Wilson to Harold Laski, from Samuel
Taylor Coleridge to Paul Elmer More, Burke vanquished
Paine in this debate; and certainly he won the immense
majority of his countrymen, so that Britain turned all her
energies toward the defeat of revolutionary violence. The
leadership which is inspired by honor, that love of things
established which grows out of a veneration of the wisdom
of our ancestors, that sagacity which reconciles necessary
change with the best in the old order—these things Burke
knew to be superior to the pretended Rights of Man that
Paine extolled; and British and American society have been
incalculably influenced by Burke ever since the *Reflections*
was published.[9]

On first examination, the *Reflections* may seem to be a
loose-knit book; but really it is nothing of the sort. Burke
"winds into his subject like a serpent," blending history
with principle, splendid imagery with profound practical
aphorisms. All his life, he detested "abstractions"—that is,
speculative notions with no secure foundation in history or
in knowledge of the world. What Burke is doing in this
book, then, is to set forth a system of "principles"—by
which he meant general truths obtained from the wisdom
of our ancestors, practical experience, and a knowledge of
the human heart. He never indulges in "pure" philosophy
because he will not admit that the statesman has any right
to look at man in the abstract, rather than at particular men
in particular circumstances.

The first portion of the book is a comparison of the political convictions of Englishmen with those of the French revolutionaries. Burke demolishes Dr. Price, and proceeds to show that the Glorious Revolution of 1688 was not a radical break with English traditions, but rather a preservation of prescriptive institutions. Then he passes on to expose the sophistries and fallacies of the French reformers, and to analyze the rights of men, true and false.

Burke defends the church against the zealots of Reason, and the old constitution of France against the fanatic advocates of turning society inside out. He speaks up for honor and the unbought grace of life. Then, in the latter portion of his tract, he assails the National Assembly, which by presumption has been delivered up to folly and crime, and which will end by ruining justice and terminating its own existence.

Written at white heat, the *Reflections* burns with all the wrath and anguish of a prophet who saw the traditions of Christendom and the fabric of civil society dissolving before his eyes. Yet his words are suffused with a keenness of observation, the mark of a practical statesman. This book is polemic at its most magnificent, and one of the most influential political treatises in the history of the world.

Few books have had so immediate and so enduring an influence, indeed—as Walter Scott observed. "About 1792, when I was entering life, the admiration of the god-like system of the French Revolution was so rife, that only a few old-fashioned Jacobites and the like ventured to hint a preference for the land they lived in," Scott wrote, in 1831, or pretended to doubt that the new principles must be infused into our worn-out constitution. Burke appeared, and all the gibberish about the superior legislation of the French dissolved like an enchanted castle when the destined knight blows his horn before it.[10]

Although more copies of Paine's reply were sold than of the *Reflections,* Burke captured, soon or late, the minds of the English and Scottish writers of the rising generation, so that his indirect influence was incalculable. Walter Scott's romances are shot through and through with Burke's convictions; while Wordsworth, Coleridge, Southey, and other poets became Burke's disciples.

Nowadays, political debate is sufficiently dreary— blighted by cant, slogan, and arid commonplace. Even though the fountains of the great deep are broken up, the political rhetoric of the twentieth century is enfeebled, and—at least in America and Britain—scarcely equal in style to the daily newspaper.

It was not so in Burke's day. In the latter half of the eighteenth century, the rhetoric of politics possessed true power and subtlety. As in the age of Cicero, political speaking and writing then formed the most extensive province of the realm of humane letters. The very demagogue, such as Wilkes, was splendid as orator and pamphleteer; today he has lost his tongue.

And Burke endures, though the other political polemicists of that time are nearly forgotten. Paine has a following still: with interesting archaism, the village atheist continues to pass out paperback copies of *The Age of Reason.* Radicalism having passed Paine by long ago, the twentieth century does not turn to him for political wisdom—merely for brilliant examples of what James Boulton accurately calls "the vulgar style" of political rhetoric.[11] The enormous immediate popularity of Paine's rejoinder, Boulton suggests, was produced by the simplicity of Paine's argument and by a rhetorical method calculated to make Paine appear a plain man of the people, full of homely allusions. Yet this very simplicity now makes Paine's pamphlets shallow. As Boulton puts it,

> However astute Paine's motives in 1791, *The Rights of Man* does not give the reader the same degree of permanent pleasure that he experiences from reading the *Reflections;* Paine cannot command that complex subtlety of style and sensitivity to the resources of language displayed by Burke.[12]

Unlike Paine, Burke did not hope to reach directly the mass of Englishmen. At best, he wrote for what he called the real nation—that is, some four hundred thousand citizens, qualified by education, profession, or substance to take some part in public affairs. And he expected to be read by only a fraction of this select body: he appealed to a cultural aristocracy, as did Samuel Johnson.

As a contemporary wrote, Burke reasoned in metaphor. Evoking images, Burke sought to persuade by his appeal to the moral imagination—not by setting his own abstractions against the abstractions of the *philosophes.* As Boulton observes, the most significant and persuasive portion of the *Reflections* is the apostrophe to Marie Antoinette— not the "philosophical center" of that book, Burke's refutation of the revolutionary concept of the social contract.

Abhorring the "abstract metaphysician," the merciless
rationalist, Burke was not attempting a systematic treatise
on political theory, after the fashion of William Godwin.
Enduring political wisdom, both practical and theoretical,
runs through Burke's speeches and tracts; but Burke's
method is a world away from that of the Encyclopedists.

For all that, Burke outmatched the French doctrinaires
at their own appeal to reason. His central argument on the
nature of the rights of men is sufficient illustration. The
French revolutionaries talked incessantly of abstract and
misty "rights of man," universal and imprescriptible.
Burke retorted that practical civil liberty is quite different
from these amorphous concepts:

> Far am I from denying in theory, full as far is my
> heart from withholding in practice (if I were of power
> to give or to withhold) the *real* rights of men. In
> denying those false claims of right, I do not mean to
> injure those which are real, and are such as their
> pretended rights would totally destroy. If civil soci-
> ety be made for the advantage of man, all the advan-
> tages for which it is made become his right. It is an
> institution of beneficence, and law itself is only be-
> neficence acting by a rule. Men have a right to live by
> that rule; they have a right to do justice as between
> their fellows, whether their fellows are in politick
> function or in ordinary occupation. They have a
> right to the fruits of their industry; and to the means
> of making their industry fruitful. They have a right to
> the acquisitions of their parents; to the nourishment
> and improvement of their offspring; to instruction in
> life, and to consolation in death. Whatever each man
> can separately do, without trespassing upon others,

he has a right to do for himself, and he has a right to a fair portion of all which society, with all its combinations of skill and force, can do in his favour. In this partnership all men have equal rights; but not to equal things. He that has but five shillings in the partnership, has as good a right to it, as he that has five hundred pounds has to his larger proportion.But he has not a right to an equal dividend in the product of the joint stock; and as to the share of power, authority, and direction which each individual ought to have in the management of the state, that I deny to be amongst the direct original rights of man in civil society; for I have in my contemplation the civil social man, and no other. It is a thing to be settled by convention.

If civil society be the offspring of convention, that convention must be its law. That convention must limit and modify all the descriptions of constitution which are formed under it. Every sort of legislative, judicial, or executory power, are its creatures....

Government is not made in virtue of natural rights, which may and do exist in total independence of it; and exist in much greater clearness, and in a much greater degree of abstract perfection: but their abstract perfection is their practical defect. By having a right to every thing they want every thing. Government is a contrivance of human wisdom to provide for human *wants*. Men have a right that these wants should be provided for by this wisdom. Among these wants is to be reckoned the want, out of civil society, of a sufficient restraint upon their passions. Society requires not only that the passions of individuals should be subjected, but that even in the mass and body as well as in the individuals, the inclinations of

men should frequently be thwarted, their will controlled, and their passions brought into subjection.
This can only be done *by a power out of themselves;*
and not, in the exercise of its function, subject to that
will and to those passions which it is its office to bridle
and subdue. In this sense the restraints on men, as well
as their liberties, are to be reckoned among their
rights.

Only in a state governed by constitution, convention,
and prescription can the rights—or the aspirations—of
men be realized. Rousseau's disciples destroy the frame-
work which makes possible the chartered rights of men,
and so reduce men to anarchy or slavery—including ser-
vitude to their own passions, for "men of intemperate
mind never can be free; their passions forge their fetters."[13]
Wavering Whig peers learned from Burke that they
must set their faces against the Revolution, or see all order
uprooted and all property in peril of confiscation; the
Anglican clergy—two-thirds of whom, by Burke's esti-
mate, had smiled hesitantly upon events in France—were
taught that religion and manners could not survive
Jacobinism. Peers and parsons had read Virgil and Cicero,
and often a good deal besides; and upon them Burke's
metaphors and imagery worked powerfully, as did his
practical reasoning. When they moved, so did the nation,
despite all that Paine and Mackintosh and Wollstonecraft
and the other counter-pamphleteers could say.
The twentieth-century leader of party cannot address
himself to so coherent an aristocracy of culture as did
Burke. The contemporary politician thinks that he must
move the masses; yet he does not successfully employ a

vigorous vulgar rhetoric like that of Paine. Even the political tracts of our time aspire, at most, to the "sober, honest,
plain-speaking but temperate" method of Mackintosh (in
James Boulton's phrases), calculated to influence the middle
classes. The clichés of daily journalism, unrelieved by wit,
are the sum and substance of most political oratory in this
hour—even among those politicians with some reputation
for learning.

Early in the nineteenth century, according to Burke's
most ardent American disciple, John Randolph of Roanoke,
one could quote to Congressmen only Shakespeare and
the Bible, if one desired the signs of recognition. That was
nearly a century and a half ago: Shakespeare and the
Authorized Version might not always be evocative in
Senate and House today, nor in the House of Commons.

Burke's *Reflections* did pass beyond the comparatively
small audience which he had expected; but to reach a wide
public, even at the end of the eighteenth century, it was
necessary to abridge the book, with judicious deletions.
Boulton draws attention, for instance, to the popular
misunderstanding of Burke's phrase "the swinish multitude," referring to the fate of learning when a revolution
should sweep away the natural guardians of culture, and
which "was used by Burke to denote the unthinking,
uncultivated masses, the irresponsible elements in society
whose lack of involvement in sustaining the cultural heri-
tage would lead them to destroy it." This passage, widely
misinterpreted or misunderstood, and fiercely attacked,
was omitted by Burke's abridger, "S.J.," in 1793, for "it
would prove either repugnant or unintelligible to poorer
readers."[14]

In the age of one-man, one-vote, any such striking phrase, however true, is the more liable to partisan attack and popular resentment or bewilderment. Thus the political orator or pamphleteer in the twentieth century tends to confine himself to platitudes which few will challenge, and to avoid words tending toward that "obscurity" with which Paine charged Burke. By such blandness, most of the time, elections are won; but the language of politics suffers—and often the public welfare suffers, too, since an impoverished and timid vocabulary means impoverished and timid political action.

But Burke's vocabulary of politics resulted in action far from impoverished or timid; even today, Burke's words are rallying cries. Today the pertinence of the *Reflections* is greater for both conservatives and liberals (Burke himself was both) than it was half a century ago. The revolutions of our times have dissipated the shallow optimism of the early years of the nineteenth century. Having broken with the old sanctions to integrity, Burke wrote, revolutionaries must come down to terror and force, the only influences which suffice to govern a society that has forgotten prudence and charity.

The spirit of religion and the spirit of a gentleman, Burke declared, gave to Europe everything generous and admirable in modern culture. A speculative system which detests piety, manners, the traditional morality, and all ancient usages speedily must repudiate even the pretended affection for equality which gives that innovating system its initial appeal to the masses.

All the decent drapery of life is to be rudely torn off.
All the superadded ideas, furnished from the ward-

robe of a moral imagination, which the heart owns and the understanding ratifies, as necessary to cover the defects of our naked, shivering nature, and to raise it to dignity in our own estimation, are to be exploded, as a ridiculous, absurd, and antiquated fashion.

On this scheme of things, a king is but a man, a queen is but a woman, a woman is but an animal— and an animal not of the highest order.... On the scheme of this barbarous philosophy, which is the offspring of cold hearts and muddy understandings, and which is as void of solid wisdom as it is destitute of all taste and elegance, laws are to be supported only by their own terrors, and by the concern which each individual may find in them from his own private speculations, or can spare to them from his own private interests. In the groves of *their* academy, at the end of every vista, you see nothing but the gallows.

Nineteenth-century meliorists took for mere distempered fancy the preceding paragraph, once the French Revolution was over; but in truth, Burke was describing the necessary character of all ideologies, or armed doctrines. To our sorrow, we dwell (except for those of us who are temporarily secure upon virtual islands of refuge in the modern flood) in the twentieth-century "antagonist world" of madness, discord, vice, confusion, and unavailing sorrow that Burke contrasted with the just civil social order, founded on conscientious leadership and prescriptive institutions.

A year after the *Reflections* was published, the ascendancy of that book was not yet complete among Burke's old friends of the Rockingham-Fitzwilliam connection, though by 1793 the power of Burke's mind, combining with the reaction against the Terror in Paris, would turn the bulk of thinking Englishmen toward plans for striking a counter-blow at Jacobinism. Even Earl Fitzwilliam, cast (with some flaws) in Rockingham's mold, still hoped, late in 1791, that a clash with Continental radicalism might be averted; he hesitated to enlist in a crusade against the revolutionary regime. (Like Rockingham before him, Fitzwilliam had been extending large financial assistance to Burke; when Fitzwilliam seemed to dissent in part from Burke's convictions on this point, the hard-pressed statesman, declining in health and deprived of many friends, nevertheless resolutely told the Earl that he would accept no more such help from him—and offered to give up his parliamentary seat at Malton.)

By 1793, however, the pamphlets of Paine and Priestley, the sermons of Dr. Price, the intrigues of the Constitutional Society and the Revolutionary Society, even the eloquence of Fox, all were scattered like chaff in the blast of Burke's whirlwind wrath. "I am come to a time of life," he wrote to Lord Fitzwilliam,

> in which it is not permitted that we should trifle with our existence. I am fallen into a state of the world, that will not suffer me to play at little sports, or to enfeeble the part I am bound to take, by smaller collateral considerations. I cannot proceed, as if things went on in the beaten circle of events, such as I have known them for half a century.[15]

To save men from silly little catechisms of rights without duties; to save them from ungovernable passions aroused by filling men with aspirations that cannot be gratified in nature; to save men from sham and cant—that was Burke's endeavor in his assault upon the *philosophes* and the Jacobins. In truth, it was Burke, not Napoleon, who laid the fell spirit of innovation which was bestriding the world. Abstract doctrine and theoretic dogma had made the Revolution; Burke evoked the wisdom of the species to restrain the hard heart of the "pure metaphysician." Human nature is a constant, and the metaphysicians of the Enlightenment could not make man and society anew: they could only ruin the constructions of thousands of years of painful human endeavor.

"We," he wrote of the English,

> are not the converts of Rousseau; we are not the disciples of Voltaire; Helvétius has made no progress amongst us.... We know that *we* have made no discoveries, and we think that no discoveries are to be made, in morality; nor many in the great principles of government, nor in the idea of liberty, which were understood long before we were born, altogether as well as they will be after the grave has heaped its mould upon our presumption, and the silent tomb shall have imposed its law upon our pert loquacity.

As Louis Bredvold comments upon this passage,

> Politics then, according to Burke, ought to be adjusted, not to bare human reason, but to human nature, of which reason is but a part, and, he adds, by no means the greatest part. Burke could not have conceived of a nation or a people or a community as anything like a collection of machines in a factory, all

> beautifully adjusted and synchronized by a system of
> belts and transmissions, regulated by human engi-
> neering; neither would he believe that human felicity
> could be found in any anarchic state of society. To
> form a good and humane society, Burke thought,
> many things are necessary, in addition to good laws;
> he emphasized the importance of religion, traditions
> of living, a rich heritage of customs, a complex pat-
> tern of relationships of all kinds, such as would not
> only develop the personality of the individual—to
> use the popular phrase of our day—but which would
> also teach him the truth about his own nature by
> their discipline of him.[16]

At bottom, the difference of Burke from the revolutionaries—like all large differences of opinion—was theological. Burke's was the Christian understanding of human
nature, which the men of the Enlightenment violently
rejected. We must leave much to Providence; to presume
to perfect man and society by a neat "rational" scheme is
a monstrous act of *hubris*. With his friend Johnson, Burke
abided by Christian resignation—and Christian hope.

To the revolutionaries, Christianity was superstition—
and an enemy. The dogmas and doctrines of Christianity
must go by the board. But in short order, theological
dogmas were supplanted by secular dogmas. Christian
charity was supplanted by "fraternity"—which, in effect,
led to the attitude "Be my brother, or I must kill you." The
Christian symbols of transcendence were adapted to the
new order, but in a degraded form: for perfection through
grace in death, the French theorists substituted the promise of perfection in this world, with every appetite satisfied.

And when perfection was not promptly attained, wicked obscurants and reactionaries must be hunted down, for Progress surely would triumph, were it not for ignorant or malicious human obstruction.

Thus arose the "armed doctrine," an inverted religion, employing central political power and strength of arms to enforce conformity to its "rational" creed. Through destruction of ancient institutions and beliefs, the way must be cleared to Utopia. Since Burke's day, the label "ideology" has been affixed to what he called "the armed doctrine"—political fanaticism, promising general redemption and idyllic general happiness to be achieved through radical social alteration.

But Utopia never will be found here below, Burke knew; politics is the art of the possible, not of perfectibility. We never will be as gods. Improvement is the work of slow exploration and persuasion, never unfixing old interests at once. Mere sweeping innovation is not reform. Once immemorial moral habits are broken by the rash Utopian, once the old checks upon will and appetite are discarded, the inescapable sinfulness of human nature asserts itself: and those who aspired to usurp the throne of God find that they have contrived a terrestrial Hell.

For seven years, Burke contended against the Jacobin heresy. Danton demanded to behold "the bronze seething and foaming and purifying itself in the cauldron"—that is, society in white-hot ferment, every impurity burnt out. But Danton was consumed in his own revolutionary cauldron. Burke knew that the just society is nothing like a cauldron; on the contrary, society is a spiritual corporation, formed by a covenant with the Author of our being:

Each contract of each particular state is but a clause in the great primeval contract of eternal society, linking the lower with the higher natures, connecting the visible and invisible world, according to a fixed compact which holds all physical and all moral natures each in their appointed place. This law is not subject to the will of those, who, by an obligation above them, and infinitely superior, are bound to submit their will to that law. The municipal corporations of that universal kingdom are not morally at liberty at their pleasure, and on their speculations of a contingent improvement, wholly to separate and tear asunder the bonds of their subordinate community, and dissolve it into an unsocial, uncivil, unconnected chaos of elementary principles.

In 1790, it appeared that the ancient states of Europe were dissolving into the dust and powder of an atomic age; generation would not link with generation, men would be as the flies of a summer, and whole classes would be proscribed and hunted down like beasts. "What shadows we are, and what shadows we pursue!" Burke had said, ten years before, on declining the poll at Bristol. What one man might do to resist this disintegration, Burke would undertake.

In 1805, William Wordsworth, abjuring the radicalism of his youth, asked the dead Burke's pardon for his early errors. The lines of *The Prelude* describe Burke in 1791:

> *I see him,—old, but vigorous in age,—*
> *Stand like an oak whose stag-horn branches start*
> *Out of its leafy brow, the more to awe*
> *The younger brethren of the grove,...*

> *While he forewarns, denounces, launches forth*
> *Against all systems built on abstract rights,*
> *Keen ridicule; the majesty proclaims*
> *Of Institutes and Laws, hallowed by time;*
> *Declares the vital power of social ties*
> *Endeared by Custom; and with high disdain,*
> *Exploding upstart Theory, insists*
> *Upon the allegiance to which men are born....*

To Coleridge, also, once he had renounced his Gallic enthusiasm, Burke's moral imagination became the source of poetic truth. As Coleridge wrote in his ode on France, in 1798:

> *The Sensual and the Dark rebel in vain,*
> *Slaves by their own compulsion!*

This is the spirit, and almost the phrase, of Edmund Burke, whom the rising generation heard, and not in vain.[17]

8

The Defense of Civilization

From the hour when he had first taken his seat in Parliament, Edmund Burke had been an advocate of peace: conciliation with the American colonies, generous concession in Ireland, repudiation of British aggrandizement in India. But from 1790 onward, he demanded war to the knife against the European revolutionaries, going beyond Pitt and the cabinet in his sternness.

There existed no alternative to war, he cried; Britain must triumph over fanaticism, or all Europe would fall to the enemies of the just civil social order, and Britain must share in that ruin. For an "armed doctrine" cannot rest: with all the ferocious enthusiasm that characterizes heretics in their early vigor, the French revolutionaries were bent upon establishing a universal domination of their secular dogmas; conquest and subversion were their instruments. No one can make peace with those whose ambitions are limitless, and for whom violence is forever necessary that they may rouse public support and conceal the practical failure of their own gloomy system.

Here, initially, he differed with most men of mark in his own party. Sir Gilbert Elliot, William Windham, French Laurence, and some of the younger men followed him steadily, from the publication of the *Reflections* onward; but Portland, Fitzwilliam, and the other Whig magnates of his connection were most uneasy at Burke's demand for militant action against the revolutionaries; while Fox and all his followers vehemently disagreed with their former colleague, believing that a brave new world was discernible across the Channel. His tremendous book was more applauded by Tories and former adversaries: Horace Walpole praised the *Reflections* wholeheartedly; Gibbon even assented to Burke's pages on religion! But those who detested the *Reflections* raised a howling storm of counter-pamphlets, and among the polemicists, at first, Burke seemed isolated.

Yet he was undeterred by his literary foes, or by the sneers and interruptions of the Foxite Whigs in the House of Commons. In May, 1791, he published his *Letter to a Member of the National Assembly*, replying to a moderate French critic of the *Reflections*. This second tract was a virtual declaration of war: since the rightful leaders of France could not regain authority by themselves, Burke argued, the fanatics of the Revolution must be put down by force from without.

The ideologues of the Revolution, he reasoned, lived by fraud, and would continue to deceive the French people by promises that they could not fulfill. Besides, the revolutionary leaders positively enjoyed the violence they had initiated:

> The life of adventurers, gamesters, gypsies, beggars, and robbers is not unpleasant. It requires restraint to keep men from falling into that habit. The shifting tides of fear and hope, the flight and pursuit, the peril and escape, the alternate famine and feast of the savage and the thief, after a time render all course of slow, steady, progressive, unvaried occupation, and the prospect only of a limited mediocrity at the end of long labour, to the last degree tame, languid, and insipid. Those who have been once intoxicated with power, and have derived any kind of emolument from it, even though but for one year, never can willingly abandon it. They may be distressed in the midst of all their power; but they will never look to anything but power for their relief.

Thus the revolutionaries, far from turning moderate, would proceed to further proscription, compulsion, confiscation, and centralization, if not arrested by force; they really meant to march on to their secular Zion. What else might be expected of the disciples of Jean-Jacques Rousseau, "the insane Socrates of the National Assembly?" "Rousseau is a moralist or he is nothing." The moral system of Rousseau impels them to stamp out the resistance of Christian morality and constitutional authority.

Like a false religion, a false morality cannot tolerate a true. Only the genuinely religious spirit maintains the rule of law; and while that spirit survives, no tyrant and no band of radical oligarchs can rest secure. The good citizen has a "holy function"; but the New Morality of the revolutionaries loathes civic holiness.

Burke's words here, says John MacCunn,

must sound extravagant to secular minds, to whom
politics altogether is nothing more than a matter of
most mundane business, and very far indeed from
being 'holy.' But they are not the less on that account
significant of the civil importance of religion as understood by one of the greatest of all its exponents.
Reverently religious in his own life, convinced by his
diagnosis of human nature that man is 'a religious
animal,' and insistent always that religious institutions are an organic element in the body-politic, it
was inevitable that Burke should recoil from a merely
secular citizenship as unequal to the demands and
burdens which the State imposes on its members. To
them it can only seem a devout imagination. But they
can be in no doubt, if they have read his pages, that
to leave this aspect out would make his political
message a wholly different, and, in his eyes, an impoverished thing.[1]

Rousseau and his pupils exalt egoism, in private and in
public life, as the essence of their new morality, Burke
pointed out. Bestowing a kiss upon the universe, actually
they neglect personal obligations and "the little platoon we
belong to in society."

Their great problem is to find a substitute for all the
principles which hitherto have been employed to
regulate the human will and action. They find dispositions in the mind of such force and quality as may
fit men, far better than the old morality, for the
purposes of such a state as theirs, and may go much
further in supporting their power and destroying
their enemies. They have therefore chosen a selfish,
flattering, seductive, ostentatious vice, in the place of

plain duty. True humility, the basis of the Christian system, is the low, but deep and firm foundation of all real virtue. But this, as very painful in the practice, and little imposing in the appearance, they have totally discarded. Their object is to merge all natural and all social sentiment in inordinate vanity.

And vanity leads to crime. Voltaire, Helvétius, and Rousseau had labored to extinguish that fear of God which is the beginning of wisdom.

The revolutionaries' abstract idealism—as Charles Parkin suggests in his commentary on this point of Burke's—leads to an intolerant moral absolutism: fanaticism has no resting-place short of Heaven—or Hell. Quite as Burke had spent his career in opposition to political absolutism, he now denounced the moral absolutism of Rousseau, "a lover of his kind, but a hater of his kindred." Parkin observes that Burke transcended the politics of empiricism in his crusade against the Revolution:

> The repudiation of its moral absolutism forms the deepest impulse in Burke's hatred of the Revolution, and constitutes the ground of his condemnation of the movement in its entirety, irrespective of minor evils which it may remove or minor goods which it may produce. The abstract idealism to which it appeals is itself the worst offense against morality, that is, against the real moral order. Morality is something to be perceived and acknowledged by human beings, not conceived by them as an image of their best selves. Abstract idealism reduces itself to an assertion of will, and will is not a creative moral force; on the contrary, its dominance is a breach of the moral order....

The unnatural passions not only oust the natural affections,

Parkin continues,

but fabricate an artificial morality. Thus, the new French morality, Burke argues, is producing a decline in the quality of feeling and a general degradation of taste. The passion of love has always hitherto had a recognized quality and a moral worth, which gave grace and nobleness to the natural appetites. The new French system is replacing this with the moral principles of Rousseau, which infuse a ferocious blend of pedantry and lewdness, of metaphysical speculations blended with the coarsest sensuality. This is the substitution, for a natural delicacy and restraint, of an artificial prudery, which in censuring the expression of natural feelings gives freedom to the unnatural. It is an unholy alliance of puritanism and primitivism. A hardening of hearts accompanies a relaxing of morals.[2]

The legend that Burke once was an unsuccessful candidate (against Adam Smith) for the professorship of moral philosophy at Glasgow University seems to have no foundation; but Burke might have made a name for himself in that discipline, had he ever found time to turn away from politics. As Ross Hoffman observes, Burke took his first principles from the Authorized Version of the Bible and the Book of Common Prayer. Like Samuel Johnson, he could not abide those who disingenuously argue that men have neither innate knowledge of moral matters nor any moral authority in the experience of the human race. And his detestation of Rousseau was very like Johnson's.

Christian humility, Burke continued, was supplanted in France by "the ethics of vanity." In the name of a sentimental love of humanity, Rousseau's votaries destroy all the old obligations of children to parents, servants to masters, citizens to magistrates. This caricature of true love is a cloak for government by terror and extirpation of all who oppose the Revolution.

"Statesmen like your present rulers," Burke told his French critic,

> exist by everything which is spurious, fictitious, and false; by everything which takes the man from his house and sets him on a stage; which makes him up an artificial creature, with painted, theatric sentiments, fit to be seen by the glare of candlelight, and formed to be contemplated at a due distance. Vanity is too apt to prevail in all of us and in all countries.... But it is plain that the present rebellion was its legitimate offspring, and it is piously fed by that rebellion with a daily dole.

With the educational system of Rousseau, and the false politics it produces, a nation can compromise only to its imminent peril. In the name of humanitarian sentiments, the revolutionaries plan a sanguinary absolutism. They have only begun to attack; soon they will go further. In defense of true social affection, legitimate authority must take prompt measures to crush "the ethics of vanity" and the tyranny produced by it; for they never will love where they ought to love who do not hate where they ought to hate.

In the eyes of some of his closest colleagues, Burke had

gone too far in the *Reflections.* Philip Francis, when that book was published, had sent him a supercilious letter full of mockery. Always warmhearted, Burke made every effort to retain Francis' friendship (though it might have been better for Burke had they never met).

"You are the only friend I have who will dare to give me advice," he replied to Francis.

> I must have then, something terrible in me, which intimidates all others who know me from giving me the only unequivocal mark of regard. Whatever this rough and menacing manner may be, I must search myself upon it; and when I discover it, old as I am, I must endeavour to correct it....

Francis had advised him to abstain from controversy with Dr. Price, Lord Shelburne, and their circle. "I should agree with you about the vileness of the controversy with such miscreants as the Revolution Society and the National Assembly," Burke answered on this point,

> and I know very well that they as well as their allies the Indian delinquents will darken the air with their arrows. But I do not yet think they have the advowson of reputation, I shall try that point. My dear Sir, you think of nothing but controversies, 'I challenge into the field of battle and return defeated.' If their having the last word be a defeat, they most assuredly will defeat me, but I intend no controversy with Dr. Price or Lord Shelburne or any of their set. I mean to set in a full View the danger from their wicked principles and their black hearts, I intend to state the true principles of our constitution in Church and State, upon grounds opposite to theirs.... I mean to do my

best to expose them to the hatred, ridicule, and contempt of the whole world, as I shall always expose such calumniators, hypocrites, sowers of sedition, and approvers of murder and all its triumphs. When I have done that, they may have the field to themselves and I care very little how they triumph over me since I hope they will not be able to draw me at their heels and carry my head in triumph on their poles.[3]

The *Letter to a Member of the National Assembly,* going beyond the *Reflections* in its condemnation of the Revolution, terminated the intimacy of men like Francis. And as for Charles James Fox—of whom (in his last days) Burke said, "He is made to be loved"—he stood at the opposite pole from Burke. On April 15, 1791, Fox had told the House of Commons that the new French constitution was "the most stupendous and glorious edifice of liberty which had been erected on the foundation of human integrity in any time or country." On May 6, during a debate on Canadian government, the Foxite Whigs mocked Burke when he began to discuss the revolution in France. The gulf had opened among the Whigs; Fox, knowing this, wept as he replied to Burke, for their friendship was at an end. Horace Walpole describes that occasion:

> ...The Prince of Wales is said to have written a dissuasive letter to Burke; but he was immovable; and on Friday, on the Quebec Bill, he broke out, and sounded a trumpet against the plot, which he denounced as carrying on here. Prodigious clamour and interruption arose from Mr. Fox's friends; but he, though still applauding the French, burst into tears and lamentations on the loss of Burke's friend-

ship, and endeavoured to make atonement; but in vain, though Burke wept too. In short, it was the most affecting scene possible; and undoubtedly *an unique* one, for both the commanders were in earnest and sincere.[4]

Fox's faction proceeded to read Burke out of the party; and indeed Burke thought himself almost friendless among the Whigs, whatever applause he received from the clergy, the country gentlemen, and former opponents. He replied to Fox's group in a powerful pamphlet published in August, 1791: *An Appeal from the New to the Old Whigs.* Fox and all his followers, Burke thundered, were subverting government by their doctrine that "the people" may make and unmake governments at their passing pleasure. He reminded his readers of the Whig doctrine of 1688: once a nation has settled upon a covenant, that contract cannot be altered by a temporary alleged majority.

> And the votes of a majority of the people, whatever their infamous flatterers may teach in order to corrupt their minds, cannot alter the moral any more than they can alter the physical essence of things. The people are not to be taught to think lightly of their engagements to their governours; else they teach governours to think lightly of their engagements towards them. In that kind of game, in the end, the people are sure to be losers.

Men with a relish for arbitrary power encourage the crowd in such delusions. This led Burke to expound his theory of social contract and duty. Many of our duties are not voluntary; they are prescribed by the moral law; by "a divine tactic," God has assigned to every man a certain condition, and has given men duties.

> When we marry, the choice is voluntary, but the duties are not matter of choice: they are dictated by the nature of the situation. Dark and inscrutable are the ways in which we come into the world. The instincts which give rise to this mysterious process of nature are not of our making. But out of physical causes, unknown to us, perhaps unknowable, arise moral duties, which, as we are able perfectly to comprehend, we are bound indispensably to perform. Parents may not be consenting to their moral relation; but, consenting or not, they are bound to a long train of burdensome duties towards those with whom they have never made a convention of any sort. Children are not consenting to their relation; but their relation, without their actual consent, binds them to its duties; or rather it implies their consent, because the presumed consent of every rational creature is in unison with the predisposed order of things.

So it is with men in community: whether individuals like it or not, they lie under moral obligation to obey the laws and sustain the state. A mere temporary majority of men, told by the head, have no right to destroy the whole constitution on a whim. The majority is leaderless and given to error, unless it accepts the role of a nation's natural aristocracy:

> A true natural aristocracy is not a separate interest in the state, or separable from it. It is an essential integrant part of any large body rightly constituted. It is formed out of a class of legitimate presumptions,

which, taken as generalities, must be admitted for
actual truths. To be bred in a place of estimation; to
see nothing low and sordid from one's infancy; to be
taught to respect one's self; to be habituated to the
censorial inspection of the public eye; to look early to
public opinion; to stand upon such elevated ground
as to be enabled to take a large view of widespread and
infinitely diversified combinations of men and affairs
in a large society; to have leisure to read, to reflect,
and converse; to be enabled to draw the court and
attention of the wise and learned, wherever they are
to be found; to be habituated in armies to command
and to obey; to be taught to despise danger in the
pursuit of honour and duty; to be formed to the
greatest degree of vigilance, foresight, and circumspection, in a state of things in which no fault is
committed with impunity and the slightest mistakes
draw on the most ruinous consequences; to be led to
a guarded and regulated conduct, from a sense that
you are considered as an instructor of your fellow-
citizens in their highest concerns, and that you act as
a reconciler between God and man; to be employed
as an administrator of law and justice, and to be
thereby among the first benefactors to mankind; to
be a professor of high science, or of liberal and in-
genuous art; to be amongst rich traders, who from
their success are presumed to have sharp and vigorous understandings, and to possess the virtues of
diligence, order, constancy, and regularity, and to
have cultivated an habitual regard to commutative
justice: these are the circumstances of men that form
what I should call a *natural* aristocracy, without
which there is no nation.

The French revolutionaries, and the "New Whigs," would reduce society to a primitive condition, by destroying such a natural aristocracy. "Art is man's nature"; but the disciples of Rousseau fall into the foolish notion that somehow primitive man was happier and better, because more "natural," than civilized man. That way lies madness.

The *Appeal* pleased the King and many others; but still Portland, Fitzwilliam, Charlemont, and other leaders of the Whigs did not come forward to support Burke vigorously. Burke had the instincts of the English people—even of the Tory mob—at his back; yet he could move neither the government nor the opposition. As James Mackintosh—Burke's ablest opponent in the pamphlet-war that followed publication of the *Reflections*—commented on this in 1804:

> The opposition mistook the moral character of the revolution; the ministers mistook its force: and both parties, from pique, resentment, pride, habit, and obstinacy, persisted in acting on these mistakes after they were disabused by experience. Mr. Burke alone avoided both these fatal mistakes. He saw both the malignity and the strength of the revolution. But where there was wisdom to discover the truth, there was not power, and perhaps there was not practical skill, to make that wisdom available for the salvation of Europe.[5]

By this time, Burke was almost conducting his own foreign policy. Throughout Europe, he was known as the foremost opponent of the Revolution—though nearly everyone abroad overestimated Burke's practical influence in English politics. (At home, during this period, Burke was admired even by those who detested his attitude toward the Revolution; his reputation as a man of ideas never had stood higher; yet he could not much move those in power, until the drift of events reinforced his arguments.) At the request of the exiled French statesman Calonne, Burke sent his son Richard to Coblenz, on the Rhine, to consult with the fugitive French princes, and Burke himself corresponded with two future kings of France; but nothing could be accomplished. In adversity—as another conservative of genius, Chateaubriand, discovered—the Bourbons were not prudent, nor yet very valiant. Burke outlined to his son what the Bourbon princes ought to guarantee:

> They ought to promise distinctly and without ambiguity, that they mean, when the monarchy, as the essential basis, shall be restored, to secure with it a free constitution; and that for this purpose, they will cause, at a meeting of the states, freely chosen, according to the ancient legal order, to vote by order, all *Lettres de Cachet,* and other means of arbitrary imprisonment, to be abolished. That all taxation shall be by the said states, conjointly with the king. That responsibility shall be established, and the public revenue put out of the power of abuse and malversation; a canonical synod of the Gallican church to reform all abuses; and (as unfortunately the king has lost all reputation) they should pledge themselves, with their lives and fortunes, to support, along with their king, those conditions and that wise order, which can alone support a free and vigorous government. Without such a declaration, or to that effect, they can hope for no converts. For my part, for one, though I make no doubt of preferring the an-

cient course, or almost any other, to this vile chi-
mera, and sick man's dream of government, yet I
could not actively, or with a good heart and clear
conscience, go to the re-establishment of a monar-
chical despotism in the place of this system of anarchy.[6]

It is clear that Burke was far from being an unqualified
admirer of the Old Regime; his plan of reform on the
pattern of the English constitutional monarchy, with parliamentary government, was admirable; but the vengeful
princes at Coblenz were in no mood to clothe it with flesh.
Burke worked hard upon the ministry in London for strong
action: the British government must come to the aid of the
exiles and of the European states imperiled by revolutionary France, for the French frenzy transcended frontiers,
and England was not safe.

These arguments were forcefully expressed in his
Thoughts on French Affairs (December, 1791), explaining
how the Revolution was one of "doctrine and theoretic
dogma," comparable to the religious movements of the
Reformation, and similarly provoking military conflict.
The Germanys, Switzerland, Italy, Spain, Sweden, Russia,
Poland, the Low Countries, and even England were in
danger of subversion, for the radicals centered in Paris
took advantage of every discontent to foment risings. He
described the character of the revolutionary plot, and the
tactics of the revolutionaries. Burke concluded with a
passage which some scholars, very curiously, have inter-
preted as a mark of feebleness in Burke. What is to be done
to prevent the conquest of Europe by fanaticism? Burke
asks. Not possessing power, he could not answer ad-

equately: "The remedy must be where power, wisdom, and information, I hope, are more united with good intentions than they can be with me." He had done what he could.

> If a great change is to be made in human affairs, the minds of men will be fitted to it, the general opinions and feelings will draw that way. Every fear, every hope, will forward it; and then they who persist in opposing this mighty current in human affairs will appear rather to resist the decrees of Providence itself than the mere designs of men. They will not be resolute and firm, but perverse and obstinate.

Leo Strauss interprets this passage to mean that Burke would yield the pass to any "progressive" movement of vast power:

> Burke comes close to suggesting that to oppose a thoroughly evil current in human affairs is perverse if that current is sufficiently powerful; he is oblivious of the nobility of last-ditch resistance. He does not consider that, in a way which no man can foresee, resistance in a forlorn position to the enemies of mankind, 'going down with guns blazing and flag flying,' may contribute greatly toward keeping awake the recollection of the immense loss sustained by mankind, may inspire and strengthen the desire and the hope for its recovery, and may become a beacon for those who humbly carry on the works of humanity in a seemingly endless valley of darkness and destruction.... We are here certainly at the pole opposite to Cato, who dared to espouse a lost cause.[7]

Now certainly Burke was deeply discouraged when he concluded the *Thoughts,* for he seemed to stand in solitary defiance of the French Revolution. But his sentences do not mean that he was preparing the way for surrender. Burke frequently said that Providence may be retributory, as well as beneficent. The loss of America, Burke thought, might be a divine punishment for British misrule in India; but one does not volunteer to be an instrument of a retributory Providence against one's own country. Also Burke still thought it possible that men's minds might be moved by Providence to resist the Revolution; he was endeavoring to be a Providential instrument of that cause. Strauss scarcely seems to be aware that Burke was demanding, in the *Thoughts,* an assault "with guns blazing" on revolutionary France; Burke *was* the "last-ditch resistance." Like Cato at Utica, Burke would not have chosen to survive the triumph of the enemies of freedom.

Pitt's ministry was not persuaded by the *Thoughts*: on January 31, 1792, the King's Speech ignored France altogether. Pitt clung tenaciously to non-intervention. The French declaration of war against Austria did not alter the ministry's policy: instead, Britain declared formal neutrality. But by late spring, the increased ferocity of the revolutionary movement—predicted by Burke a year and a half earlier—alarmed many in England; moreover, the Allies had done little against revolutionary France. Portland, Fitzwilliam, and the other Old Whigs began to move, slowly, in Burke's direction.

On May 11, in the course of the debate on the petition of the Unitarians to be relieved of their disabilities (Burke considering the Unitarians of that day to be a subversive political sect, rather than a true religious body), Burke crossed the floor of the House of Commons to signify his complete disagreement with Fox, then and on later occasions so acting to suggest that the Portland Whigs should go into coalition with the Pitt government. "He squeezed himself in between Dundas and Pitt."[8]

Burke's prophecies in the *Reflections,* meanwhile, were being fulfilled. The Parisian mob stormed the Tuileries on August 10, slaughtered the Swiss Guard, and took the royal family as prisoners; that Burke had expected. Danton, who desired to boil France in a cauldron, and who was the best swaggering example of Rousseau's "New Morality," now dominated the Revolution. There followed the French victory over the Prussians at Valmy, and the September Massacres in the prisons of Paris. Members of the ministry took alarm at the propaganda, in England, of Paine and his radical associates. Burke now drew up a systematic paper for the ministers to weigh, *Heads for Consideration on the Present State of Affairs.*

In this document, Burke was military analyst and architect of grand strategy. He urged Pitt's government to form, without delay, an offensive alliance of all the monarchies and old republics of Europe: it was not enough to save monarchs; the nations of Europe must be liberated from the Jacobins, and in France the monarchy must be restored. The French royalists still in arms, and the French *émigrés,* should be employed as the vanguard of liberating armies, backed by British might; Britain, indeed, rather than Austria, should assume the general command of this tremendous campaign.

In vague reply, Pitt and Grenville inquired whether Burke could persuade the Old Whigs to join with them; he tried, but still the Whig magnates vacillated, not wishing to alienate Fox. In Parliament, by December, the principal antagonists were Burke and Fox—though the two still were engaged jointly in the prosecution of Hastings.

Country gentlemen of the Old Whig persuasion—more than seventy, perhaps—in the House of Commons now were commencing to follow Burke into some degree of support for the government. By January, 1793, some of the really influential Whigs, most notably Lord Malmesbury, crossed to the government benches. In February, Burke and forty-four others resigned from the Whig Club, dominated by the Foxites.

Fox and the pro-French Whigs had lost. On January 21, 1793, the revolutionaries took off the head of Louis XVI, King of France; thus they fulfilled Burke's prediction of their limitless ferocity. At this murder, George III sent the French ambassador packing. Diplomatic relations severed, France invaded Holland (a British ally) and proposed to take control of the river Scheldt; on February 1, the Convention declared war on England. Willy-nilly, Pitt's government had lost its neutrality.

Burke thought it grimly absurd that, after these years of pulling and tugging in Parliament, and while the abyss of Hell yawned, at last Britain should go to war, tardily, over a question of the navigation of the Scheldt. "A war for the Scheldt!" he exclaimed. "A war for a chamber pot!" But at least Britain now must confront fanaticism boldly. Pitt said he expected victory to be obtained after a campaign or two; Burke replied that the war would be long and weary work.

By summer, the government was overwhelmingly strong in the House of Commons. Portland, Fitzwilliam, and their set still declined to enter into coalition with Pitt; but they found it difficult to criticize Burke, for his definition of the "Old Whig" was precisely what they considered themselves to be.

In June, the Mountain proscribed the Girondins in the Convention. Danton was slipping toward his destruction; Robespierre, incorruptible and pursuing a deadly "virtue," was engaged in the extirpation of all opposition. In his *Remarks on the Policy of the Allies with respect to France,* written in the autumn, Burke asked that the war become a crusade for the restoration of order throughout Europe, not merely a military policy to advance British interests (which latter point of view still was Pitt's). It was to be a war against the usurpers of power, not against the French people; the natural proprietors of the land would be restored. It was impossible to come to terms with the Jacobins (and some voices in the ministry were said to be whispering of just that possibility), for the Jacobins would respect no treaty. It was a religious war—a war intended by the Jacobins to destroy all religion, Catholic or Protestant:

> In all that we do, whether in the struggle or after it, it is necessary that we should constantly have in our eye the nature and character of the enemy we have to contend with. The Jacobin Revolution is carried on by men of no rank, of no consideration, of wild, savage minds, full of levity, arrogance, and presumption, without morals, without probity, without prudence. What have they, then, to supply their innumerable defects, and to make them terrible even to the firmest minds? One thing, and one thing only— but that one thing is worth a thousand: they have energy. In France, all things being put into a universal ferment, in the decomposition of society, no man

comes forward but by his spirit of enterprise and the vigour of his mind. If we meet this dreadful and portentous energy, restrained by no consideration of God or man, that is always vigilant, always on the attack, that allows itself no repose, and suffers none to rest an hour without impunity; if we meet this energy with poor commonplace proceeding, with trivial maxims, paltry old saws, with doubts, fears, and suspicions, with a languid, uncertain hesitation, with a formal, official spirit, which is turned aside by every obstacle from its purpose, and which never sees a difficulty but to yield to it, or at best to evade it— down we go to the bottom of the abyss, and nothing short of Omnipotence can save us. We must meet a vicious and distempered energy with a manly and rational vigour.

He proceeded to outline a plan for restoring order to France and the rest of Europe after victory, emphasizing the need for a strong France in the comity of nations; this must not be a war merely to secure advantage and reparations for England. While he wrote, the Allies were making headway against the Jacobin forces; his friend Elliot was at Toulon, from which naval base the British hoped to thrust toward the centers of French power; the French royalists were fighting manfully in Brittany. Had Burke's counsels of strategy been followed in detail, the Jacobins might have been broken in 1793 or 1794, and two decades of destruction would have been averted. But at that hour, imagination and conviction were lacking in the English government and among the Allies generally, and the opportunity was lost.

For the Jacobins had only begun to fight; Burke had been

accurate in his analysis of the need for a different sort of military undertaking by the Allies. Even as Burke wrote, the Republic's armies prepared a fresh offensive; they took Toulon from the British in December. Then the French pushed into the German states, the Netherlands, and Spain, smashing the Allied forces.

The grave plight of Britain at this disastrous moment, combined with Burke's repeated approaches to Portland and other leading Old Whigs, persuaded Portland, Fitzwilliam, and their colleagues, at last, to enter into coalition with Pitt (May, 1794), taking six of the thirteen posts in the cabinet. Exhausted, Burke himself sought no office. He had vindicated himself as a true Whig: Fox and his followers were reduced to an impotent rump of the Whig party. The prosecution of Hastings was in its last stage, and Burke applied for the office of warden of the Chiltern Hundreds, then as now the formal step for retirement from Parliament. Near the end of June, 1794, Burke's three decades of eminence in the House of Commons came to an end.

He, far more than anyone else, had set in motion the forces that would undo Jacobinism, so that in future times men would refer to "Burke and the French Revolution" as if these were equal, though opposite, powers. But he was perhaps thirty thousand pounds in debt, with a regular annual income of only five hundred pounds. In a time when many politicians of every faction had accumulated massive fortunes from office or political connection, Burke had served country and party, not himself—so that unless relieved somehow, he might actually have to go abroad to escape his creditors, or else end in a debtors' prison.

Pitt and the King rescued him, granting him a pension of two-thousand five-hundred pounds a year, for his life and that of his wife; on the strength of this, enough money was raised to satisfy the more pressing creditors, and Gregories did not have to be sold. Sixty-five years old, Burke withdrew to Beaconsfield—but not to obscurity. To the last, he would use his pen against Jacobinism, urging the prosecution of the war upon a plan very different from Pitt's. The concluding three years of his life were to be a time of consuming sorrow and consuming activity.

9

*Never Succumb
to the Enemy*

In a country house crammed with impecunious and sickly Irish kinfolk, refugee Frenchmen, and dependents of divers sorts, Edmund Burke maintained to his last day the cause of justice in society, contending against Jacobin usurpation and striving to improve the lot of the Irish. "Justice is itself the great standing policy of civil society," he had said, "and any eminent departure from it, under any circumstances, lies under the suspicion of being no policy at all." For all his support of Pitt, as against Fox, he thought that the Pitt ministry had small interest in justice for Europe or Ireland.[1]

Only a scrap survives today of the estate of Gregories, near the placid old town of Beaconsfield.[2] The fine house burnt after Mrs. Burke sold it: a fatality has overtaken many of the places Burke knew. At Gregories, Burke directed a nearby school (with a government subsidy) for the children of French *émigré* families; he sheltered, or sustained by gifts and loans, a crowd of fugitives from the Jacobin terror, until sometimes he had scarcely a guinea for himself, and had to borrow again; and he was a power in the world, despite his lack of office and of money.

His brother Richard was dead now; so were most other men whom he had loved—Reynolds, Johnson, Goldsmith, Garrick; Fox, Sheridan, and others were forever parted from him; Will Burke was ruined and dying. No sooner had he retired from the House of Commons, than he was afflicted by a loss that struck him more sorely than all the rest: his only son, Richard (to whom Fitzwilliam had given the Malton parliamentary seat that had been the father's), died of tuberculosis. Now Burke's family would be extinguished, and posterity would know him only through his words. His grief at the loss of Richard was terrible and inconsolable. In his *Letter to a Noble Lord,* he compared himself with Job:

> The storm has gone over me; and I am like one of those old oaks which the late hurricane has scattered about me. I am stripped of all my honours, I am torn up by the roots, and lie prostrate on the earth! There, and prostrate there, I most unfeignedly recognize the divine justice, and in some degree submit to it.

At this juncture, he was attacked in the House of Lords by the Duke of Bedford and the Earl of Lauderdale. These peers had joined themselves to the Foxite Whigs, and expected to embarrass Burke, in his crusade against the Jacobins, by reproaches for his having accepted a pension from the Crown. He was false to his old principles, they said; he had fallen into the very corruption he once denounced; he was a bought man. This charge was absurd; and even had there been substance in it, Bedford and

Lauderdale were not the men to bring it. They notoriously were what old Thomas Fuller called "degenerous gentlemen": their families, the Russells and the Maitlands, had accumulated wealth beyond the dreams of avarice by undeserved grants from the Crown and political manipulation; a long history of gross opportunism tarnished both families.

Burke replied in what Woodrow Wilson considered his finest work, *A Letter...to a Noble Lord, on the Attacks made upon him and his Pension, in the House of Lords* (1796). A lesser man would have found it easy enough to overwhelm Bedford, whose ancestors—by doubtful or reprehensible means—had extracted from the Crown the enormous estates which the young Duke who accused Burke now enjoyed. Burke's literary powers being undiminished by age, the rebuke to the Duke was tremendous. Was it wrong for Burke to accept, for having done good, some tiny fraction of what Bedford's ancestor had accepted for doing duty as a sycophant? The Duke should have contented himself with saying, "I am a young man with very old pensions; he is an old man with very young pensions—that's all."

But Bedford's assault on Burke's reputation was meant, in effect, to aid the French levelers. Let the Duke look to his own security! The revolutionaries, drawing up scores of new constitutions to suit every fancy, would not spare the Duke's property, nor the Duke himself, should they make their way to arbitrary power in England. For the Jacobins, taking in vain the name of humanity, are merciless in their methods:

They are ready to declare, that they do not think two thousand years too long a period for the good that they pursue. It is remarkable, that they never see any way to their projected good but by the road of some evil. Their imagination is not fatigued with the contemplation of human suffering through the wild waste of centuries added to centuries of misery and desolation. Their humanity is at their horizon— and, like the horizon, it always flies before them. The geometricians, and the chemists, bring, the one from the dry bones of their diagrams, and the other from the soot of their furnaces, dispositions that make them worse than indifferent about those feelings and habitudes, which are the supports of the moral world. Ambition is come upon them suddenly; they are intoxicated with it, and it has rendered them fearless of the danger, which may from thence arise to others or to themselves. These philosophers consider men, in their experiments, no more than they do mice in an air pump, or in a recipient of mephitick gas.

And they would treat the Duke as if he were a mouse.

In this portrait of the leveling ideologue, who justifies every atrocity by an expected social benefit to distant futurity, Burke described the political fanatic who has plagued the world ever since 1789. The whole of this *Letter* flames with such prophetic imagery. Henry Crabb Robinson, in 1858, read the *Letter* aloud to two ladies, and then remarked to himself: "I can imagine no eloquence more perfect—that is, in composition. In style combining every variety of charm."[3] But the Duke of Bedford could not have been charmed.

English justice, Burke wrote, secures the real rights of

Englishmen against the ferocious ambitions of the revolutionaries, which would abolish at one stroke all prescription. And what of the Duke of Bedford then?

The learned professors of the rights of man regard prescription, not as a title to bar all claim, set up against all possession—but they look on prescription as a bar against the possessor and the proprietor. They hold an immemorial possession to be no more than a long continued, and therefore an aggravated, injustice.

Such are *their* ideas; such their religion, and such *their* laws. But as to our country and our race, as long as the well compacted structure of our church and state, the sanctuary, the holy of holies of that ancient law, defended by reverence, defended by power, a fortress at once and a temple, shall stand inviolate on the brow of the British Lion—as long as the British monarchy, not more limited than fenced by the orders of the state, shall, like the proud Keep of Windsor, rising in the majesty of proportion, and girt with the double belt of its kindred and coeval towers, as long as this awful structure shall oversee and guard the subjected land—so long the mounds and dykes of the low, fat Bedford level will have nothing to fear from all the pickaxes of all the levellers of France. As long as our sovereign lord the king, and his faithful subjects, the lords and commons of this realm—the triple cord, which no man can break; the solemn, sworn, constitutional frank-pledge of this nation; the firm guarantees of each other's being, and each other's rights; the joint and several securities, of property and of dignity:—as long as these endure, so long the duke of Bedford is safe; and we are all safe

> together—the high from the blights of envy and the
> spoliations of rapacity; the low from the iron hand of
> oppression and the insolent spurn of contempt. Amen!
> and so be it.

There were no more criticisms of Burke's pension. For
Burke, decayed in health and retired to the oaks of
Beaconsfield, was formidable as ever—and, to folk unlike
the Duke of Bedford, generous as ever. To him at Gregories
came diplomats, philosophers, peers, men of letters, bish-
ops, obscure unfortunates, exiled children: he found time
(and, if need be, money) for them all.

The young and then unknown Chateaubriand made his
way to Gregories, as did so many *émigrés* grateful to Burke,
and found the statesman acting as dominie to his French
schoolchildren. "I went to see what he called his 'nursery.'
He was amused at the vivacity of the foreign race which was
growing up under his paternal genius. Looking at the
careless little exiles hopping, he said to me:

"'Our boys could not do that.'

"And his eyes filled with tears. He thought of his son who
had set out for a longer exile."[4]

To Gregories, too, at Burke's last Christmas, came James
Mackintosh, author of *Vindiciae Gallicae*—the best-rea-
soned reply to Burke's *Reflections*—but since converted by
Burke and by the course of events to detestation of the
Jacobins. (Burke received him with private suspicions,
initially, but welcomed him as an ally of intellectual power.)
Mackintosh

> described, in glowing terms, the astonishing effu-
> sions of his mind in conversation: perfectly free from

all taint of affectation; he would enter, with cordial
glee, into the sports of children, rolling about with
them on the carpet, and pouring out, in his gambols,
the sublimest images, mingled with the most wretched
puns. —Anticipated his approaching dissolution
with due solemnity but perfect composure;—minutely and accurately informed, to a wonderful ex-
actness, with respect to every fact relative to the
French Revolution.

From the systematic Mackintosh, this was high praise
indeed; yet he had higher still, speaking of Burke

with rapture, declaring that he was, in his estimation,
without any parallel, in any age or country, except,
perhaps, Lord Bacon and Cicero; that his works
contained an ampler store of political and moral
wisdom than could be found in any other writer
whatsoever; and that he was only not esteemed the
most severe and sagacious of reasoners, because he
was the most eloquent of men, the perpetual force
and vigour of his arguments being hid from vulgar
observation by the dazzling glories in which they
were enshrined.[5]

One product of the old Burke's wisdom, during this
period, was the foundation of the seminary for Irish
Catholics at Maynooth, in which Burke had a large hand.
Maynooth was meant to elevate the intellects of the Irish
priests, so helping to save Ireland from Jacobinism; and
very much had Maynooth been needed. Though Burke
failed in his attempt to place control of the college entirely
in the hands of the Catholic clergy, its establishment with

governmental approval and participation was Burke's final success in his war upon the Penal Laws.

At death's door, Burke was more powerful than ever he had been before; yet Britain was in sore peril as he watched his French children and wrote his last tracts at Gregories. The war against the Revolution went badly. Instead of invading France in force, Pitt kept a quarter of a million soldiers idle in England, while he gobbled up the French colonies in the West Indies. Even now, Pitt and Dundas were not wholly convinced that Jacobinism must be ground to powder, lest it rise again; they talked of coexistence. When Prussia dropped out of the Armed Coalition against France, and Austria faltered, Pitt told Malmesbury that, "as an English minister and a Christian," he meant to end "this bloody and wasting war." Within the cabinet, it was now the Old Whigs, led by Portland, Windham, Fitzwilliam, and Loughborough, who were wholly won to Burke's convictions and so demanded victory, whatever its cost, over the enemies of European order.[6]

With Robespierre fallen, might not the hard-eyed men who dominated the latest stage of the Revolution be brought to see reason? Britain might make large concessions to them, for the sake of peace. The Foxites clamored for a settlement with the Directory; Pitt and the Tory ministers in the coalition squinted that way.

In this doubtful moment, Burke began writing his concluding philippics against the ideologues of France, his four *Letters on a Regicide Peace,* two of which were not published until after his death. His predictions of the dreadful course of the Revolution had been fulfilled almost to the letter: Marie Antoinette had died on the scaffold—

the heroic queen of whom Burke had written, in 1790, that she bore her misfortunes "with a serene patience, in a manner suited to her rank and race...." The Revolution had ravaged Europe, and devoured many of its own children; but the sanguinary appetite of the revolutionaries was insatiable. Should Britain come to terms with murderers and brigands, who meant to subdue Britain, too, by subversion and conquest?

Burke's answer was a ringing negative; and events soon justified him. In Paris, the Directory masqueraded as a constitutional government, but actually was a thorough tyranny; the Directors never truly meant to make peace with Pitt, but only played for time. So Burke told Fitzwilliam in a formal memorandum meant for official eyes only, but which was never completed, though eventually published— in 1812—as the "Fourth" *Letter on a Regicide Peace*. (Actually, it was Burke's first treatment of this subject.) Remarkably good-humored and witty, clearly meant to persuade rather than to excoriate the Pitt government, this "Fourth" Letter was a reply to Lord Auckland's pamphlet advocating negotiations with the Directory. It had become impossible to restore monarchy, church, and nobility in France, Auckland argued; one must settle for the possible, and French radicalism had so far diminished that one might think of acceptable terms.

Burke answered (Christmas, 1795) that such a policy would amount to surrender, destroying the government, the Crown, and the country. Burke never had been more cogent. E. J. Payne considers this paper, and its sequels, to be the peer of the *Reflections,* and in some respects a better work:

> In the 'Reflections' Burke was avowedly writing in
> a partial and prejudiced sense. He took upon himself
> to expound on the spur of the moment the unrea-
> soned creed and the traditional sentiment of the
> ordinary Englishman of his day. In the [*Regicide
> Peace*] Burke relinquishes this 'John Bull' masquer-
> ade, and writes as a statesman, a scholar, and an
> historical critic. The reader will find more than one
> of his earlier arguments repudiated. This was the
> natural result of wider and more prolonged experi-
> ence.[7]

The "First" and "Second" Letters (chronologically, the
second and third letters) were written at the urging of the
Portland Whig members of the ministry, when Pitt seemed
to be on the verge of suing for peace, and were published
in October, 1796. By the time Burke's tract appeared, Pitt
had made his approaches to the Directory—and had been
humiliatingly rebuffed: for France would not give up the
Austrian Netherlands, and Britain could not abandon her
principle of a balance of power in Europe which should
keep French ambitions within bounds. The "Third" Letter
was written (though published only posthumously, in
November, 1797) after the failure of Lord Malmesbury's
further negotiations for peace, rejected by the Directory in
December, 1796.

The theme of the *Regicide Peace* is the necessity for
making an end of Jacobinism, root and branch. In his *Letter
to William Smith* (January, 1795) Burke had written,

> What is Jacobinism? It is the attempt (hitherto but
> too successful) to eradicate prejudice out of the minds
> of men, for the purpose of putting all power and

authority into the hands of persons capable of occasionally enlightening the minds of the people. For this purpose the Jacobins have resolved to destroy the whole frame and fabric of the old societies of the world, and to regenerate them after their fashion. To obtain an army for this purpose, they everywhere engage the poor by holding out to them as a bribe the spoils of the rich.

It was the duty of Britain to redeem Europe from this heresy—which was slavery—Burke maintained in his *Regicide Peace*. For this purpose, a just war—long and costly, though (as he made clear in the Third Letter) Britain could defray the expense—must be waged. In international law, the war was justified: it was as if a neighbor had set up at one's own door a menace and a nuisance, which anyone was entitled to remove. Wars may be wrong and violent; but also they may be "the sole means of justice among nations"; everything depends upon the purpose. He never would advocate a "mercenary war." (Here Burke implied that Pitt was carrying on just such a mercenary conflict, which, as wits then said, would make Pitt master of every island in the world—except the British Isles.)

The calculation of profit in all such wars [for material gain] is false. On balancing the account of such wars, ten thousand hogsheads of sugar are purchased at ten thousand times their price. The blood of man should never be shed but to redeem the blood of man. It is well shed for our family, for our friends, for our God, for our country, for our kind. The rest is vanity; the rest is crime.

But Britain should wage war unrelentingly upon the Jacobins, for indeed the blood of man then would be shed to redeem the blood of man. The Jacobins were bent upon ruining the Christian commonwealth of Europe,

> virtually one great state, having the same basis of general law, with some diversity of provincial customs and local establishments. The nations of Europe have had the very same Christian religion, agreeing in the fundamental parts, varying a little in the ceremonies and in the subordinate doctrines. The whole of the policy and economy of every country in Europe has been derived from the same sources.

Jacobinism was a general evil, not merely a local one; so what was being fought was a civil war, not a foreign war.

> It is a dreadful truth, but it is a truth that cannot be concealed: in ability, in dexterity, in the distinctness of their views, the Jacobins are our superiors. They saw the thing right from the beginning. Whatever were the first motives to the war among politicians, they saw that in its spirit, and for its objects, it was a *civil* war; and as such they pursued it. It is a war between the partisans of the ancient civil, moral and political order of Europe against a sect of fanatical and ambitious atheists which means to change them all. It is not France extending a foreign empire over other nations: it is a sect aiming at universal empire, and beginning with the conquest of France. The leaders of that sect secured *the centre of Europe;* and that secured, they knew that, whatever might be the event of battles and sieges, their *cause* was victorious.

The survival of European civilization being at stake,

Britain must strike at the heart of Jacobin power, in France. Should Jacobinism be allowed to retain the core of the European commonwealth, in time Jacobinism would triumph everywhere—including Britain. Although only a fifth of the real political public of England and Scotland (out of the four hundred thousand men capable of forming political opinions) inclined toward the Jacobin creed, these would become effective revolutionaries and assume power, should Britain be so weak as to make peace with the French Jacobins. Jacobinism does not rely upon numbers, but upon tight organization and fanatic belief. As Burke had said repeatedly in the course of his career, it is sufficient for the triumph of evil that good men should do nothing.

> Jacobinism is the revolt of the enterprising talents of a country against its property. When private men form themselves into associations for the purpose of destroying the pre-existing laws and institutions of their country; when they secure to themselves an army, by dividing amongst the people of no property the estates of the ancient and lawful proprietors; when a state recognizes those acts; when it does not make confiscations for crimes, but makes crimes for confiscations; when it has its principal strength, and all its resources, in a violation of property; when it stands chiefly on such a violation; massacring by judgments, or otherwise, those who make any struggle for their old legal government, and their legal, hereditary, or acquired possessions—I call this *Jacobinism by establishment.*

With such fanatics, compromise and concession avail not at all; the Jacobins will temporize when it seems to their advantage, but will resume their assault so soon as the friends of order and justice are off their guard.

> To them the will, the wish, the want, the liberty, the toil, the blood of individuals, is as nothing. Individuality is left out of their scheme of government. The state is all in all. Everything is referred to the production of force; afterwards, everything is trusted to the use of it. It is military in its principles, in its maxims, in its spirit, and in all its movements. The state has dominion and conquest for its sole objects: dominion over minds by proselytism, over bodies by arms.

Burke was describing here the pattern of ideological despotism all too familiar to us, nearly two centuries later, after experience of the Nazis and the Communists and other political sectaries. To combat such an armed doctrine, Britain must abandon the tactics of previous contests for power. "We have not considered as we ought the dreadful energy of a state in which the property has nothing to do with the government...where nothing rules but the mind of desperate men." By propaganda and terror, the masters of such a total state can prevent any successful rising against their total oppression; only intervention by a free nation, employing all its resources and faith with a force and spirit equal to that of the radical oligarchy, can work emancipation of countries already fallen under the despotic yoke. The Jacobin state must be destroyed, or "it will destroy all Europe.... In one word, with this republic nothing independent can coexist."

The latter part of the *Regicide Peace* was published only after Pitt had found that the Directory would not make peace with Britain, in any event, except on terms that would amount to English surrender. These tracts' influence, therefore, was on the politicians and writers of the rising generation—Canning, Frere, and their friends, for instance—rather than upon the coalition ministry which Burke addressed.

So the war went on to Waterloo; and—what almost no one except Burke and Fitzwilliam had thought possible—the prolonged English assault on French radicalism in its several forms did accomplish, in 1815, the overthrow of despotism in Europe and the partial restoration of the European commonwealth, with its religion, its laws, and its private rights. More than in any other cause which he upheld, Burke succeeded in this defense of European civilization—though long after his death.

On March 30, 1797, from Bath—where he was seeing what the waters could do for his emaciated body, tormented by tuberculosis and perhaps cancer—Burke wrote to William Windham that as matters were drifting, the nation must suffer defeat; the ministry's fiscal, diplomatic, and military policies were timorous. Pitt "cannot make peace, because he will not make war. He will be beaten out of all his entrenchments. The enemy is turning his flanks."[8]

That year of 1797, indeed, was one of staggering reverses for Britain. The fleets at Spithead and the Nore mutinied—as Burke had suggested they might—and the mutineers were put down only after an agonizing glimpse of possible national ruin. Napoleon swept triumphantly through Italy; Austria withdrew from the war; the Bank of England suspended specie payment. Yet Burke still trusted in Providence. When almost done, he told his friends to fight on:

> Never succumb to the enemy; it is a struggle for your existence as a nation; and if you must die, die with the sword in your hand; there is a salient, living principle of energy in the public mind of England which only requires proper direction to enable her to withstand this or any other ferocious foe; persevere till this tyranny be overpast.[9]

In these final years, he had given to mankind what once he gave to party. On the night of July 9, 1797, Burke died at Gregories. He had worked to his last day. Fox, forgiving everything, wished to have the body interred in Westminster Abbey, but Burke had chosen the old church at Beaconsfield for his burial; and somewhere there his bones lie.

Madame D'Arblay—Fanny Burney, that is—was present at Burke's funeral; and a passage from her subsequent letter to her father, Dr. Burney, Burke's old friend (who had spoken at the funeral), may serve as a candid epitaph for Edmund Burke. She had reason to like Burke, for once he had paid her the greatest compliment that a busy statesman might, by sitting up all night to read her novel *Evelina.*

> How sincerely I sympathize in all you say of that truly great man! That his enemies say he was not perfect is nothing compared with his immense superiority over almost all those who are merely exempted from his peculiar defects. That he was upright in heart, even where he acted wrong, I do truly believe...and that he asserted nothing he had not persuaded himself to be true, from Mr. Hastings's being the most rapacious of villains, to the King's being incurably insane. He was as generous as kind,

and as liberal in his sentiments as he was luminous in intellect and extraordinary in abilities and eloquence. Though free from all little vanity, high above envy, and glowing with zeal to exalt talents and merit in others, he had, I believe, a consciousness of his own greatness, that shut out those occasional and useful self-doubts which keep our judgment in order, by calling our motives and our passions to account.[10]

What is very rare with public men, Burke increased steadily in reputation and influence for a great while after his death. George Canning wrote at the time, "There is only one piece of news, but it is news for the world, Burke is dead."[11] With others of both wings of the Tory party, Canning took Burke for his mentor in nearly everything. "'With Mr. Burke's last works and words still the manual of my politics,' he perpetually translated Burke's teaching into the language of practical life for the Commons or his Liverpool constituents."[12]

Thus the spokesman for the Old Whigs had reinvigorated the Tories. Yet in the generosity and courage of the old Toryism, which John Henry Newman defined as "loyalty to persons," Burke always had been as much a Tory as Samuel Johnson. Yeats, in his poem "The Seven Sages," touches on this, in the discourse of his seven old men:

> The Fifth. Burke was a Whig.
> The Sixth. Whether they knew it or not,
> Goldsmith and Burke, Swift and the Bishop of Cloyne,
> All hated Whiggery; but what is Whiggery?
> A levelling, rancorous, rational sort of mind
> That never looked out of the eye of a saint
> Or out of drunkard's eye.[13]

Despite his appeal to the principles of 1688, Burke had little in common with John Locke, and still less with the New Whigs. His passage on the true contract of eternal society, in the *Reflections,* illustrates how far removed he was, in first principles, from the latter-day Whig politics of rationalism. Society is indeed a contract of partnership, Burke says; but nothing like a mere commercial agreement.

> As the ends of such a partnership cannot be obtained in many generations, it becomes a partnership not only between those who are living, but between those who are living, those who are dead, and those who are yet to be born.

It is a partnership in all science, and all art. The real social compact is with God. Such language would make most Whigs, from John Locke to Thomas Babington Macaulay, not a little uneasy.

God willed the state, Burke declared, for man's benefit; men must not venture to trade upon the petty bank and capital of their private rationality, but should venerate where they do not presently understand, and abide by the wisdom of their ancestors, the winnowed and filtered experience of the human species. Life being short and experience limited, the individual—even the wisest man of his age—is comparatively foolish; but through the experience of man with God, and through the experience of man with man, over thousands of years, the species has a wisdom, expressed in prejudice, habit, and custom, which in the long run judges aright.

This faith is at the antipodes from the sort of Whiggery

that Yeats assailed. The "levelling, rancorous, rational sort of mind," the mind of the "sophisters, economists, and calculators" whom Burke detested, never would quote from memory, as did Burke, this passage from Richard Hooker:

> The reason first why we do admire those things which are greatest, and second those things which are ancientest, is because the one are the least distant from the infinite substance, the other from the infinite continuance, of God.

The party which Burke, with Rockingham, had forged to maintain the constitution fell into ruin under the impact of the French Revolution. Yet without his having expected it, after his death Burke became the intellectual founder of a new and more powerful party, the Conservative—a fusion of Tories and conservative Whigs—which now endures as the oldest coherent political party in the fluctuating twentieth-century world.*

Though this might be distinction enough for any man, it is only a lesser aspect of the achievement of Burke. His influence, with the defeat of Napoleon, spread far beyond Britain to most of western Europe, and the architects of European reconstruction lived by his maxims, to the best of their understanding. Directly or by a kind of intellectual osmosis, he permeated American political thought and action. He enlivened political philosophy by the moral imagination; he shored up Christian doctrine; he stimulated the higher understanding of history; he enriched English literature by a mastery of prose that makes him the

---

* For the essence of Burke's conservatism, see Appendix A.

Cicero of his language and nation. And to the modern civil social order, he contributed those principles of ordered freedom, preservation through reform, and justice restraining arbitrary power, which transcend the particular political struggles of his age. Against the fanatic ideologue and the armed doctrine, the great plagues of our time, Burke's wisdom and Burke's example remain a powerful bulwark.

The philosopher in action, Burke knew, can alter the whole course of nations, for good or ill. We are not governed by mere Fate and Fortune; no inexorable destiny rules nations. "I doubt whether the history of mankind is yet complete enough, if ever it can be so, to furnish grounds for a sure theory of the internal causes which necessarily affect the fortune of a State." The ways of Providence are mysterious, but we need not bow down before theories of historical determinism, which a twentieth-century writer, Gabriel Marcel, calls "that armed ghost, the 'meaning' of history."

Private thoughts and individual actions, Burke pointed out in the Fourth Letter of the *Regicide Peace,* may alter profoundly the apparent great drift of the times.

> The death of a man at a critical juncture, his disgust, his retreat, his disgrace, have brought innumerable calamities on a whole nation. A common soldier, a child, a girl at the door of an inn, have changed the face of fortune, and almost of Nature.[14]

Burke himself, in his almost solitary opposition of 1790, did incalculably much to exorcise the revolutionary spirit of the age, which his most enlightened contemporaries had mistaken for the irresistible genius of the future.

The prophecies of the Jacobins and their kind, Burke understood, are of the sort which work their own fulfillment—if honest men credulously accept the ideologue's dogmatic assertions. But if possessed of principle, resolution, and moral imagination, men may unite to restrain the enemies of order and justice and freedom. To precisely that unending labor of curbing arbitrary will and arbitrary appetite, Burke devoted his life. Because corruption and fanaticism assail our era as sorely as they did Burke's time, the resonance of Burke's voice still is heard amidst the howl of our winds of abstract doctrine.

Epilogue

Why Edmund Burke
Is Studied

Cato the elder told his friends, "I had rather that men should ask, 'Why is there no monument to Cato?' than that they should ask, 'Why is there a monument to Cato?'" Now I do not suppose that people often inquire, "Why is there a monument to Burke in the city of Washington?" Nevertheless, some Americans in high places remain interestingly ignorant of the great men and women whose statues loom tall in L'Enfant's little parks; therefore, in considering Edmund Burke's statue I offer you some reflections on why Burke is still much read and quoted nowadays.

Statues have their enemies, a sept of that body of the malicious whom I have called, in one of my books, the *Enemies of the Permanent Things*. Three decades ago the gentleman then Secretary of the Interior declared that Washington was cluttered with monuments to nobodies—anyway, to folk forgotten by everybody—and that those statues ought to be cleared away. Pressed for an example of the nobodies he had in mind, the Secretary of the Interior responded, "Well, that statue of Benjamin Rush, whoever he was." Now Dr. Benjamin Rush, as many today are aware, was one of the more eminent signers of the Declaration of Independence; but that is not the most important thing about him. Rush was a famous physician, a man of letters, one of the two founders of the first antislavery society in America, the holder of various public offices, and a chief man of intellect during the formative years of the Republic. As one edition of the *Encyclopaedia Britannica* summarizes Rush's literary productivity:

> Benjamin Rush's writings covered an immense range of subjects, including language, the study of Latin and Greek, the moral faculty, capital punishment, medicine among the American Indians, maple sugar, the blackness of the negro, the cause of animal life, tobacco smoking, spirit drinking, as well as many more strictly professional topics. His last work was an elaborate treatise on *The Diseases of Man* (1812). He is best known by the five volumes of *Medical Inquiries and Observations,* which he brought out at intervals from 1789 to 1798 (two later editions revised by the author).

Such was the scholar and public man whose effigy the Secretary of the Interior would have consigned to Avernus. (Incidentally, that Secretary was given to frequent praise of "intellectuals.") But *nil admirari*! Earlier in this century, the administrators of New York City's parks came near to tossing into the Hudson the bronze bust of Orestes Brownson, the most vigorous of American Catholic thinkers; the bust had been knocked off its pedestal in Riverside Park, and everybody in authority had quite forgotten poor Brownson. (That bust was rescued in the nick of time by

Fordham University and may be seen on Fordham's campus today.) From ignorance or from malice, there flourishes in our era a breed of haters of the past, who chuck down the memory-hole of *1984* (the dystopia, not the literal year) everything venerable upon which they may lay their hands. Statues in particular are anathema to them. If given their way, such persons would commission junk sculpture to supplant every representation in stone or bronze of a great human being. Not long ago an agency of the federal government was eager to persuade colleges to adorn their campuses, at national expense, with "abstract sculpture," the product of the welder's torch; so far as I know, no "representational" sculpture was approved in this national program. One thinks again of Orwell's dystopia, in which the one remaining gratification is the pleasure of effacing the humane. "If you want a picture of the future," O'Brien tells Winston, "imagine a boot stamping on a human face—forever."

Men in our time—so my old friend Max Picard wrote before 1930 in his book *The Human Face*—

> fear to gaze upon the face of man. We have no wish to be reminded of the whole man, we do not wish wholeness; on the contrary, we wish to be divided, and we are pleased in our state of division and do not wish to be disturbed. For that reason we do not contemplate the human face.

Now Edmund Burke, who detested political abstractions, was no abstraction himself; he was a whole man, undivided. Being undivided, he is not loved by the zealot for a faceless egalitarian uniformity in society; nor by the enthusiast for perpetual change, the "permanent revolution." If, in the near future, this Burke statue still stands in deathless bronze on Massachusetts Avenue; and if its original by Thomas still stands at Bristol; and especially if the fine statue of Burke stands beside that of his friend Oliver Goldsmith in College Green, Dublin—why, they will remain as symbols of a human order that has not been pulled down altogether. But if those statues of Burke are one day no longer to be seen—well, their vanishing will be a sign that humankind has been expelled from what Burke called "this world of reason, and order, and peace, and virtue." Humanity will have been thrust into Orwell's dystopia—into the realm of Chaos and old Night, described by Burke as "the antagonist world of madness, discord, vice, confusion, and unavailing sorrow."

No memorial statue of Burke ever was to be found at Beaconsfield, where Burke had his house and farm. Somewhere in church or churchyard there, Burke's bones lie buried; but the precise spot is unknown. Should the Jacobins triumph in England, Burke feared, his body might be exhumed by the radicals and his head and quarters put on macabre public show, as had been done to the corpses of politicians before him; worse than that had been done to quick and dead in France during the closing years of Burke's existence. Therefore his body had been interred secretly and by night, somewhere about Beaconsfield church. That Jacobinism never seized upon Britain was the accomplishment, in considerable part, of Burke's eloquence; the "antagonist world" did not then take on substance in England.

Yet a fatality seems to have afflicted the visible memorials of Burke's life, these statues apart. Burke's birthplace on Arran Quay in Dublin, still standing uninhabited when first I strolled along the Liffey, since has been thoughtfully demolished by Dublin's municipal authorities. Soho Square, where Burke had his London residence, is turned into a loathsome hell upon earth, the equivalent of New York's Times Square; young women are whipped at lunchtime in restaurants, for the amusement of affluent men. As for the great house of Gregories, with Burke's library and collection of statuary and paintings, that was burnt a few years after Burke's death. But the high brick precinct-wall survives, near to Beaconsfield church, and (so I read somewhere) a large barn that had been Burke's—for he cultivated six hundred acres at Gregories. When last I visited Beaconsfield, I entered what had been the park of Gregories to seek for the barn. I did not find it; instead I came upon rows of little, neat, ticky-tacky houses, terraced so that, viewed from left to right, each miniature house stood a few feet higher than the house to its right. A curious sensation of *déjà vu* afflicted me. However could I have beheld this newbuilt housing scheme before? Then it came to me. Beaconsfield has become in recent decades the headquarters of Britain's film industry, and these terraces of monotonous dwellings can be pressed into service as film backgrounds. What picture had I seen that had so utilized these rather distressing manifestations of suburbia since World War II? I had it: *Fahrenheit 451*, Ray Bradbury's dystopia about book-burning. Burke's books had been burnt here, and there were bookburners aplenty among the socialist masters of the new comprehensive schools. On returning to America, I told Ray Bradbury about this unhappy concitation of the backward devils; he never had fancied, while his film was being produced in England, that it was being filmed upon the wreck of Burke's estate.

Much more, visible and invisible, has been wrecked by the advancing troops of the Antagonist World since Burke was buried secretly in 1797. A great part of old Bucharest, including three grand ancient monasteries, has been swept away by the Communist regime in Romania—to clear the way for monstrous new high-rise hives and a gigantic boulevard along which the legions of Mordor may parade. One thinks of the lines of John Betjeman:

> I have a vision of The Future, chum,
> The workers' flats in fields of soya beans
> Tower up like silver pencils, score on score;
> And Surging Millions hear the Challenge come
> From microphones in communal canteens
> 'No Right! No Wrong! All's perfect, evermore.'

The East, since Burke's day, has been swallowed up by the Antagonist World; and the West has been ravaged and harrowed, though not overcome utterly as yet. Even the quarter of Washington in which Burke's likeness stands seems on the verge of being lost to the world of reason, and order, and peace, and virtue.

Yet American society retains considerable recuperative powers; cheerfulness will keep breaking in. Such recuperation of the body politic results, in part, from the institutions that Burke praised and the principles Burke expounded— even though few Americans know anything about Burke except that somehow he "was for our side" in the Revolution.

Why is there a monument to Burke? Because he was a principal defender of that world of reason, and order, and peace, and virtue in which the United States participated, through its inheritance of civilization. Constitution, custom, convention, and prescription give society a healthy continuity, as Burke knew; and he pointed out that prudent change is the means of our preservation; he understood how the claims of freedom and the claims of order must be kept in a tolerable tension. Such truths he taught not as a closet-philosopher, but as a practical statesman and manager of party. His speeches and pamphlets were read by the men of 1776 and the men of 1787—and studied with yet closer attention after 1789. No other political thinker of their own time was better known to the American leaders than was Burke. That is one reason why the Sulgrave Institution, seventy-four years ago, presented a statue of Burke to the city of Washington.

In divers ways—some obvious, some subtle—Burke's politics and Burke's rhetoric have been woven into American modes of thought and argument, generation after generation. Let me suggest my own path to Burke.

I first encountered the name of Burke when, as a boy, I browsed through my mother's old schoolbooks. Among these was an edition of Burke's speech "On Conciliation with the Colonies," published by Scott, Foresman in 1898, "edited for school use by Joseph Villiers Denney," a professor at Ohio State University, with thorough notes and intelligent "Questions on the Literary and Rhetorical Qualities of the Speech." By "Schools" the publishers meant high schools, not universities. "On Conciliation" had nearly vanished from American high schools by the time I arrived there, and I know of no public school nowadays which prescribes the study of Burke's speeches. But my mother and her classmates seem to have been undismayed by this manual. Here and there, in her copy, my mother has written between lines, neatly, definitions of words or phrases; and on the back flyleaf is a notation, presumably with reference to the teacher's passing remarks on Burke's *The Sublime and Beautiful:* "Though we travel the world over to find the beautiful, we must carry it with us or we find it not." In 1898, when my mother was a high school senior, it was taken for granted that young people could apprehend Burke. It cannot be so taken for granted in the graduate schools of large universities today. As Burke predicted in *Reflections on the Revolution in France,* the time would come when learning would be trodden down under the hoofs of a swinish multitude—a phrase borrowed from the Gospel according to Saint Matthew, incidentally.

Courses in American history still contained references to Burke during my own high-school years, but I was more interested in a textbook's brief account of the Virginian John Randolph of Roanoke, who entered Congress as a radical, but by 1804 had become of Burke's persuasion. Later, as a graduate student at Duke University, I wrote a master's thesis about Randolph—and through studying him, became an attentive reader of Burke. Here is a specimen of Randolph on Burke, in a letter to Harmanus Bleeker written in 1814:

> My time of late has been...occupied in reading and meditating the Vth volume of Burke.... It has been an intellectual banquet of the richest viands. What a man! How like a child and an idiot I feel in compari-

son with him. Thank God! However, I can understand and relish his sublime truths and feel grateful
for the inspired wisdom which in the true spirit of
prophecy he has taught to us poor blind and erring
mortals.

Out of these studies came my first book, *John Randolph of Roanoke.* Perceiving how pervasive Burke's influence had been on either side of the Atlantic, I made that the theme of my second book, *The Conservative Mind.* I discovered, presently, how Joseph Story had woven the teachings of Burke into his famous *Commentaries on the Constitution of the United States;* how John C. Calhoun had learned much from Burke; how James Russell Lowell and other American men of letters were moved by Burke's style; how Woodrow Wilson, writing in 1901, declared himself Burke's disciple.

Near the end of the eighteenth century Burke had con-
tended against an "armed doctrine," Jacobinism, the first ideology of what was to become an age of ideological passions. By the 1940s Americans and their allies found themselves contending against fresh revolutionary ideolo-
gies. What precedent did the file afford? To what statesman of the past, what philosopher in action, might one turn for guidance in a time when the fountains of the great deep were broken up? It was this search, primarily, that brought about a strong renewal of serious interest in Burke, beginning nearly five decades ago.

During the 1950s many studies of Burke and his times were published in America and Britain; every serious peri-
odical commented upon the "Burke revival." By 1962 Clinton Rossiter noted in the second edition of his *Conservatism in America* that

> a fascinating by-product of the conservative upsurge
> of the postwar years has been the re-introduction of
> Burke as a serious thinker into courses in political
> theory at colleges throughout America.

Leaders of both American political parties began to quote
Burke; Senator Eugene McCarthy, in his *Frontiers of Democracy,* acknowledged Burke's dominant influence upon
his political principles.

The bursting out of radicalism during the later sixties
and early seventies to some extent impeded the renewal of
Burke's influence in intellectual quarters; but attention to
Burke increased once more as the disaster of war in
Indochina receded. Nowadays Burke is praised in such
journals as *The New Republic.* Even certain syndicated
columnists of today quote Burke repeatedly—a practice
confined pretty much to your servant thirty years ago.

Burke's statue on Massachusetts Avenue, in short, signi-
fies more now than it did in 1922, the year of its erection.
Then it was a reminder of the struggles during the closing
third of the eighteenth century; now it wakes us to the clash
of beliefs, political and religious, as the twentieth century of
the Christian era nears its end. Our Time of Troubles,
Arnold Toynbee instructs us, commenced in 1914; the
world has sunk more deeply into those grim difficulties
with every year that has elapsed since then. Is it conceivable
that the rising generation in America, whose schooling has
been so costly and yet so poor, may learn something valuable from the imagination and the intellect of the man of
genius whose brazen image seems to survey the stream of
traffic on Massachusetts Avenue—rather in the fashion of
the statue of the Happy Prince in Oscar Wilde's fable,

gazing forever upon the great city's inhumanity?

A little more than two hundred years ago Edmund Burke found his fortune at a stay. Out of office, with the younger Pitt entrenched as prime minister, Burke seemed ineffectual to many; his party—the first genuine political party of the English-speaking world—had suffered defeat and eclipse; his private affairs were troubled. There lay before him his impeachment of Warren Hastings, and Hastings' trial, to which bitter affairs Burke would devote the next decade of his life; this was no cheerful prospect, Burke knowing from the first that the House of Lords would not find Hastings guilty as charged. "We know that we bring before a bribed tribunal a prejudged cause," he wrote to Philip Francis on December 10, 1785.

Five years later, nevertheless, Burke (almost alone) commenced the undoing of the French Revolution; he published the most brilliant piece of political writing in the English language, began to alter the whole drift of British foreign policy, won back the clergy to the national cause, and achieved in political isolation a reputation and an influence exceeding that he had enjoyed while still a manager of party. It is this later Burke especially who attracts the interest and admiration of contemporary Americans.

Clinton Rossiter, in 1962, grew almost alarmed at the ascendancy of Burke among the thoughtful. The conservative task for Americans, Professor Rossiter argued, "calls for creation and integration, not imitation; it may call for revival of Adams, Hamilton, Calhoun, Madison, and the conservative Lincoln, but surely not for wholesale importation of Burke or de Maistre." And elsewhere he declared that the "prudent Federalists...must henceforth serve American conservatism as a kind of collective Burke."

This is curious reasoning. The Federalists have a justly important part in American political reflection, two centuries after their call for a Constitutional Convention. Yet the Federalists cannot well supplant Burke as a source of political wisdom, in part because the Federalists themselves drew upon Burke and in part because what the Federalists said is less relevant to the distresses of the world at the end of the twentieth century than is the bulk of Burke's writings after 1789.

For the Federalists were concerned, necessarily, with constructing a practical frame of government for a particular time and people, rather than with first principles of politics, applicable in some degree to any age. I do not mean that there is no advantage in deriving one's convictions from one's national ancestors. Some real continuity survives between the America of 1797, say, and the America of today. Yet the passage of the centuries does make a difference in national character and national needs. And if only homegrown products are fit for American consumption— why, we must prefer Jonathan Edwards as a theologian, say, over Saint Augustine, because Edwards was born in New England and Augustine in Roman Africa. Or—intending no disrespect—Mary Baker Eddy must supplant Jesus of Nazareth if we are to adopt Rossiter's chain of reasoning.

The Federalist Papers form a work of high political prudence, well argued and worthy of close attention still. The federal system of government, brought into existence by those politicians' arguments, has done much for the American people. As the United States slides toward centralization, the ideas of the Federalists grow still more deserving of renewal, by way of caution and check.

Yet the problems of modern society transcend simple questions of governmental structure. An appeal to the pristine purity of the Constitution of the United States will not suffice as a bulwark against the destructive power of ideology. To Burke, rather than to Washington or Hamilton or Jay or Madison or even John Adams, we must turn for an analysis of the first principles of order and justice and freedom.

As for pertinence to our present discontents, even *The Federalist Papers* cannot arouse imagination and conscience as can *Reflections on the Revolution in France* or the *Regicide Peace.* For Burke is urgently concerned with the grim continuing revolution of our time of troubles, while *The Federalist,* in essence, is an argument simply for settling the governmental arrangements of America near the end of the eighteenth century. One still can read with profit Washington's Farewell Address, the production (with Hamilton's assistance) of a strong and prudent man. But it is impossible for the United States of today to follow the counsels on foreign policy commended by President Washington at the end of his tenure: circumstances have altered irrevocably. Burke's understanding of the comity of civilized nations and his plea for combination against revolutionary fanaticism apply to the present circumstances of the United States, on the contrary: Burke is little "dated."

Being myself a disciple of the Federalists, I respect their practical wisdom. Nor am I of the opinion that political theories and institutions can be transferred abstractly, without qualification, from one land to another; I agree with Daniel Boorstin that "the American Constitution is not for export." It certainly would be impossible, and in a variety of ways undesirable, to establish in America a facsimile of eighteenth-century English society. Heraclitus and experience have taught us that we never step in the same river twice.

But Burke is not *outside* the American experience; rather, as his statue reminds us, he stands in the grander tradition and continuity—the legacy of our civilization —of which American life and character form a part. And Burke himself, helping to form American society, has been an influence upon this land and this people from the 1760s to the present. To seek political wisdom from Burke is no more exotic for Americans than it is to seek humane insights from Shakespeare or spiritual insights from Saint Paul. The founders of this Republic, after all, participated in political and legal institutions very like those that Burke defended; they shared Burke's climate of opinion; they read the books that Burke read. One does not set up William James and Josiah Royce, say, as better philosophers than Aristotle or Aquinas on the ground that the first pair were born on the western side of the Atlantic and the second pair on the eastern.

Some part of the institutions and the social order which Burke knew has passed away, quite as the America of our time is markedly different from the seaboard republic of Adams and Jefferson. Because we cannot restore—even if we would—either Georgian England or Jeffersonian America, the test of the relevance of a political philosopher to the challenges of our own time is not merely a question of whether his lot was cast in a bygone Britain or in a bygone United States.

In many respects the great American nation of today is

more like the imperial Britain of 1797 than like the isolated infant Republic of 1797. Because Burke addressed himself to matters that transcended nationality and generation, he endures as an important political thinker whom men of our time oppose to Karl Marx. Would anyone argue seriously that the writings of the Federalists, philosophically considered, may suffice to withstand the grim power of totalist ideology and to direct the affairs of this gigantic twentieth-century America, no longer insulated against the opinions and the arms of the Old World?

Burke, with his prophetic gifts, perceived the shape of things to come in this bent world of ours. His passionate refutation of leveling ideology and totalist politics has lost nothing of its force with the passing of two centuries. What he said of the Jacobins is yet more true of the Marxist ideologues of this century. "I have laid the terrible spirit of innovation which was overrunning the world." Those are the words of Napoleon, whose coming Burke predicted. Yet it was Burke, rather than Bonaparte, who in truth exorcised the fierce specter of revolutionary fanaticism.

No other statesman or writer of the past two centuries has been more prescient than was Burke. In my mother's day it was as a great rhetorician and leader of party, rather than as a man of thought and imagination, that Burke was studied. The specialization of our twentieth-century educational system intensified this division: the political historians hesitated to discuss Burke because he was a man of letters, the teachers of literature because he was a philosopher, the professors of philosophy because he was a statesman; and so round the circle. The very breadth of genius may cause neglect. Yet perhaps it has been as well that a proper understanding of Burke has been reserved for these years of ours. For once more we find ourselves in an epoch of concentration, in which thinking men and women endeavor to restore order and justice to a bewildered society. "I attest the rising generation!" Burke cried, at the end of his prosecution of Hastings. Indeed he did win over the rising generation of Britain, about the year of his death; and today's rising generation of Americans is influenced by the mind of Burke (directly or indirectly), as thirty years ago many of America's rising generation fell under the influence (directly or indirectly) of Jean-Jacques Rousseau, Burke's adversary. Burke's moral imagination may yet defeat Rousseau's idyllic imagination near the end of the twentieth century.

To suggest, in conclusion, the relevance of Burke's convictions to our present troubles, let me quote a passage from a letter of Burke, written on June 1, 1791, to the Chevalier Claude-François de Rivarol. Burke is discussing the illusions of poets and philosophers:

> I have observed that the Philosophers in order to insinuate their polluted Atheism into young minds, systematically flatter all their passions natural and unnatural. They explode or render odious or contemptible that class of virtues which restrain the appetite. These are at least nine out of ten of the virtues. In place of all these they substitute a virtue which they call humanity or benevolence. By these means, their morality has no idea in it of restraint, or indeed of a distinct settled principle of any kind. When their disciples are thus left free and guided by present feeling, they are no longer to be depended on

for good or evil. The men who today snatch the worst criminals from justice, will murder the most innocent persons tomorrow.

Amen to that. Burke's "Parisian philosophers" of two centuries gone live on as today's self-proclaimed "intellec-tuals," with their incessant talk of "compassion" and their advocacy, among other things, of the inalienable right to expand the empire of unnatural vices. From age to age we human beings fight the same battles over and over again, under banners bearing various devices. To resist the idyllic imagination and the diabolical imagination, we need to know the moral imagination of Edmund Burke. And that is why we know Burke for one of those dead who give us energy.

Appendix A

Burke's Conservatism

Edmund Burke never employed the term "conservative," because in his time it was not a noun of politics. He is, nevertheless, the principal source of modern conservative belief. It was in France, after the defeat of Napoleon, that the words *conservateur* and *conservatif* were coined to describe a concept of politics founded on the ideas of Burke: by definition, then, conservatism means Burke's politics of prudence and prescription, guarding and preserving a country's institutions. These terms passed into English politics during the 1820s, and into American political discussion during the 1840s.

On the model of Burke, a conservative statesman is one who combines a disposition to preserve with an ability to reform. The key passage from Burke describing this concept is found in his *Reflections on the Revolution in France,* in connection with his denunciation of the National Assembly. It is included here to suggest the essence of Burke's conservative politics.

Rage and phrenzy will pull down more in half an hour, than prudence, deliberation, and foresight can build up in an hundred years. The errors and defects of old establishments are visible and palpable. It calls for little ability to point them out; and where absolute power is given, it requires but a word wholly to abolish the vice and the establishment together. The same lazy but restless disposition, which loves sloth and hates quiet, directs these politicians, when they come to work, for supplying the place of what they have destroyed. To make every thing the reverse of what they have seen is quite as easy as to destroy. No difficulties occur in what has never been tried. Criticism is almost baffled in discovering the defects of what has not existed; and eager enthusiasm, and cheating hope, have all the wide field of imagination in which they may expatiate with little or no opposition.

At once to preserve and to reform is quite another thing. When the useful parts of an old establishment are kept, and what is superadded is to be fitted to what is retained, a vigorous mind, steady persevering attention, various powers of comparison and combination, and the resources of an understanding fruitful in expedients are to be exercised; they are to be exercised in a continued conflict with the combined force of opposite vices; with the obstinacy that rejects all improvement, and the levity that is fatigued and disgusted with every thing of which it is in possession. But you may object—"A process of this kind is slow. It is not fit for an assembly, which glories in performing in a few months the work of ages. Such a mode of reforming, possibly might take up many years." Without question it might; and it ought. It is one of the excellencies of a method in which time is amongst the assistants, that its operation is slow, and in some cases almost imperceptible. If circumspection and caution are a part of wisdom, when we work only upon inanimate matter, surely they become a part of duty too, when the subject of our demolition and construction is not brick and timber, but sentient beings, by the sudden alteration of whose state, condition, and habits, multitudes may be rendered miserable. But it seems as if it were the prevalent opinion in Paris, that an unfeeling heart, and an undoubting confidence, are the sole qualifications for a perfect legislator. Far different are my ideas of that high office. The true lawgiver ought to have an heart full of sensibility. He ought to love and respect his kind, and to fear himself. It may be allowed to his temperament to catch his ultimate object with an intuitive glance; but his movements towards it ought to be deliberate. Political arrangement, as it is a work for social ends, is to be only wrought by social means. There mind must conspire with mind. Time is required to produce that union of minds which alone can produce all good we aim at. Our patience will achieve more than our force. If I might venture to appeal to what is so much out of fashion in Paris, I mean, to experience, I should tell you, that in my course I have known, and, according to my measure, have co-operated with great men; and I have never yet seen any plan which has not been mended by the observations of those who were much inferior in understanding to the person who took the lead in the business. By a slow but well-sustained progress, the effect of each step is watched; the good or ill success of the first, gives light to us in the second; and so, from light to light, we are conducted with safety through the whole series. We see, that the parts of the system do not clash. The evils latent in the most promising contrivances are provided for as they arise. One advantage is as little as possible sacrificed to another. We compensate, we reconcile, we balance. We are enabled to unite into a consistent whole the various anomalies and contending principles that are found in the minds and affairs of men. From hence arises, not an excellence in simplicity, but one far superior, an excellence in composition. Where the great interests of mankind are concerned through a long succession of generations, that succession ought to be admitted into some share in the councils which are so deeply to affect them. If justice requires this, the work itself requires the aid of more minds than one age can furnish. It is from this view of things that the best legislators have been often satisfied with the establishment of some sure, solid, and ruling principle in government; a power like that which some of the philosophers have called a plastic nature; and having fixed the principle, they have left it afterwards to its own operation.

Appendix B

Burke's Personality

Of the few existing detailed sketches of Burke's private manners and personality, the best are by Fanny Burney, in her diary and letters. She was the daughter of Dr. Charles Burney, the historian of music, a close friend of Burke. She and her father knew everyone worth knowing in London, moving in a brilliant society. She became a much-admired novelist at the age of twenty-six in 1778, with the publication of *Evelina:* this book won the prompt applause of Burke, Johnson, and Reynolds. In 1793 she married a French exile, Alexandre D'Arblay. Her *Diary and Letters,* in seven volumes, is the most amusing of all English memoirs of the eighteenth century.

Burke, whom she venerated, appears often in her pages. The two following extracts suggest the remarkable charm, warmth, and wisdom which Burke manifested in private life; also they show the setting in which Burke lived.

The first extract from her journal is dated June, 1782; it records her first meeting with Burke, who was then Paymaster to the Forces in Rockingham's ministry, and apparently triumphant in politics. This occurred at the house of Sir Joshua Reynolds. At the same time, she was first introduced to Richard Burke, Edmund's brother, and the younger Richard, Edmund's son; she never took very kindly to either of the Richards, but from that day until the prosecution of Hastings commenced, she admired Edmund Burke unreservedly. This passage is reprinted without deletion.

Sir Joshua's house is delightfully situated, almost at the top of Richmond Hill. We walked till near dinner-time upon the terrace, and there met Mr. Richard Burke, the brother of the orator. Miss Palmer, stopping him, said,—

"Are you coming to dine with us?"

"No," he answered; "I shall dine at the Star and Garter."

"How did you come—with Mrs. Burke, or alone?"

"Alone."

"What, on horseback?"

"Aye, sure!" cried he, laughing; "*up and ride!* Now's the time."

And he made a fine flourish with his hand, and passed us. He is just made under-secretary at the Treasury. He is a tall and handsome man, and seems to have much dry drollery; but we saw no more of him.

After our return to the house, and while Sir Joshua and I were *tête-à-tête,* Lord Corke and my father being still walking, and Miss Palmer having, I suppose, some orders to give about the dinner, the "Knight of Plymton" was desiring my opinion of the prospect from his window, and comparing it with Mr. Burke's, as he told me after I had spoken it,—when the Bishop of St. Asaph and his daughter, Miss Georgiana Shipley, were announced. Sir Joshua, to divert himself, in introducing me to the bishop, said,

"Miss Burney, my lord; otherwise, 'Evelina.'"

The bishop is a well-looking man, and seemed grave, quiet, and sensible. I have heard much more of him; but nothing more appeared. Miss Georgiana, however, was showy enough for *two*. She is a very tall, and rather handsome girl; but the expression of her face is, to me, disagreeable. She has almost a constant smile, not of softness, nor of insipidity, but of self-sufficiency and internal satisfaction. She is very much accomplished, and her fame for painting and for scholarship, I know you are well acquainted with. I believe her to have very good parts and much quickness; but she is so full of herself, so earnest to obtain notice, and so happy in her confidence of deserving it, that I have been not less charmed with any young lady I have seen for many a day. I have met with her before, at Mrs. Pepys', but never before was introduced to her.

Miss Palmer soon joined us; and, in a short time, entered more company,—three gentlemen and one lady; but there was no more ceremony used of introductions. The lady, I concluded, was Mrs. Burke, wife of *the* Mr. Burke, and was not mistaken. One of the gentlemen I recollected to be young Burke, her son, whom I once met at Sir Joshua's in town, and another of them I knew for Mr. Gibbon: but the third I had never seen before. I had been told that *the* Burke was not expected; yet I could conclude this gentleman to be no other; he had just the air, the manner, the appearance, I had prepared myself to look for in him, and there was an evident, a striking superiority in his demeanour, his eye, his motions, that announced him no common man.

I could not get Miss Palmer to satisfy my doubts, and we were soon called down-stairs to dinner. Sir Joshua and the *unknown* stopped to speak with one another upon the stairs; and, when they followed us, Sir Joshua, in taking his place at the table, asked me to sit next to him; I willingly complied. "And then," he added, "Mr. Burke shall sit on the other side of you."

"Oh, no, indeed!" cried Miss Georgiana, who also had placed herself next Sir Joshua; "I won't consent to that; Mr. Burke must sit next me; I won't agree to part with him. Pray, come and sit down quiet, Mr. Burke."

Mr. Burke,—for him it was,—smiled and obeyed.

"I only meant," said Sir Joshua, "to have made my peace with Mr. Burke, by giving him that place, because he has been scolding me for not introducing him to Miss Burney. However, I must do it now;—Mr. Burke!—Miss Burney!"

We both half rose, and Mr. Burke said,—

"I have been complaining to Sir Joshua that he left me wholly to my own sagacity; however, it did not here deceive me."

"Oh dear, then," said Miss Georgiana, looking a little *consternated*, "perhaps you won't thank me for calling you to this place!"

Nothing was said, and so we all began dinner,—young Burke making himself my next neighbour.

Captain Phillips knows Mr. Burke. Has he or has he not told you how delightful a creature he is? If he has not, pray, in my name, abuse him without mercy; if he has, pray ask if he will subscribe to my account of him, which herewith shall follow.

He is tall, his figure is noble, his air commanding, his address graceful: his voice is clear, penetrating, sonorous, and powerful; his language is copious, various, and eloquent; his manners are attractive, his conversation is delightful.

What says Captain Phillips? Have I chanced to see him in his happiest hour? or is he all this in common? Since we lost Garrick I have seen nobody so enchanting.

I can give you, however, very little of what was said, for the conversation was not *suivie*, Mr. Burke darting from subject to subject with as much rapidity as entertainment. Neither is the charm of his discourse more in the matter than the manner; all, therefore, that is related *from* him loses half its effect in not being related *by* him. Such little sketches as I can recollect, take however.

From the window of the dining-parlour, Sir Joshua directed us to look at a pretty white house which belonged to Lady Di. Beauclerk.

"I am extremely glad," said Mr. Burke, "to see her at last so well housed; poor woman! the bowl has long rolled in misery; I rejoice that it has now found its balance. I never, myself, so much enjoyed the sight of happiness in another, as in that woman when I first saw her after the death of her husband. It was really enlivening to behold her placed in that sweet house, released from all her cares, a thousand pounds a-year at her own disposal, and—her husband was dead! Oh, it was pleasant, it was delightful to see her enjoyment of her situation!"

"But, without considering the circumstances," said Mr. Gibbon, "this may appear very strange, though, when they are fairly stated, it is perfectly rational and unavoidable."

"Very true," said Mr. Burke, "if the circumstances are not considered, Lady Di. may seem highly reprehensible."

He then, addressing himself particularly to me, as the person least likely to be acquainted with the character of Mr. Beauclerk, drew it himself in strong and marked expressions, describing the misery he gave his wife, his singular ill treatment of her, and the necessary relief the death of such a man must give.

He then reminded Sir Joshua of a day in which they had dined at Mr. Beauclerk's, soon after his marriage with Lord Bolingbroke's divorced wife, in company with Goldsmith, and told a new story of poor Goldsmith's eternal blundering.

The second extract is dated Thursday, June 18th, 1792. During the intervening decade, Miss Burney had been angered by Burke's vehemence in the prosecution of Hastings. Meeting in the drawing-room of Mrs. Crewe, at Hampstead, she and Burke were reconciled. The "Miss

F_____" referred to was Mary French, a niece of Burke's, who came over from Ireland to stay at Gregories the rest of Burke's life—and remained with Mrs. Burke until the widow died. Sir Gilbert Elliot, in April, 1793, described Miss French as "the most perfect *she-Paddy* that ever was caught." The beautiful Mrs. Crewe was a power among the Whigs, and long a friend of Burke. Miss Burney displays here her accustomed perceptivity:

After many invitations and regulations, it was settled I was to accompany my father on a visit of three days to Mrs. Crewe at Hampstead.

The villa at Hampstead is small, but commodious. We were received by Mrs. Crewe with much kindness. The room was rather dark, and she had a veil to her bonnet, half down, and with this aid she looked still in a full blaze of beauty. I was wholly astonished. Her bloom, perfectly natural, is as high as that of Augusta Lock when in her best looks, and the form of her face is so exquisitely perfect that my eye never met it without fresh admiration. She is certainly in my eyes, the most completely a beauty of any woman I ever saw. I know not, even now, any female in her first youth who could bear the comparison. She uglifies everything near her.

Her son was with her. He is just of age, and looks like her elder brother: he is a heavy, old-looking young man. He is going to China with Lord Macartney.

My former friend, young Burke, was also there. I was glad to renew acquaintance with him; though I could see some little strangeness in him: this, however, completely wore off before the day was over.

Soon after entered Mrs. Burke, Miss F_____, a niece, and Mr. Richard Burke, the comic, humorous, bold queer brother of *the* Mr. Burke, who, they said, was soon coming, with Mr. Elliot. The Burke family were invited by Mrs. Crewe to meet us.

Mrs. Burke was just what I have always seen her, soft, gentle, reasonable, and obliging; and we met, I think, upon as good terms as if so many years had not parted us.

At length Mr. Burke appeared, accompanied by Mr. Elliot.

He shook hands with my father as soon as he had paid his devoirs to Mrs. Crewe, but he returned my courtesy with so distant a bow, that I concluded myself quite lost with him, from my evident solicitude in poor Mr. Hastings' cause. I could not wish that less obvious, thinking as I think of it; but I felt infinitely grieved to lose the favour of a man whom, in all other articles, I so much venerate, and whom, indeed, I esteem and admire as the first man of true genius now living in this country.

Mrs. Crewe introduced me to Mr. Elliot: I am sure we were already personally known to each other, for I have seen him perpetually in the Managers' box, whence, as often, he must have seen me in the Great Chamberlain's. He is a tall, thin young man, plain in face, dress, and manner, but sensible, and possibly much besides; he was reserved, however, and little else appeared.

The moment I was named, to my great joy I found Mr. Burke had not recollected me. He is more nearsighted, considerably, than myself. "Miss Burney!" he now exclaimed, coming forward, and quite kindly taking my hand, "I did not see you;" and then he spoke very sweet words of the meeting, and of my looking far better than "while I was a courtier," and of how he rejoiced to see that I so little suited that station. "You look," cried he, "quite renewed, revived, disengaged; you seemed, when I conversed with you last, at the trial, quite altered; I never saw such a change for the better as quitting a Court has brought about!"

Ah! thought I, this is simply a mistake, from reasoning according to your own feelings. I only seemed altered for the worse at the trial, because I there looked coldly and distantly, from distaste and disaffection to your proceedings; and I here look changed for the better, only because I here meet you without the chill of disapprobation, and with the glow of my first admiration of you and your talents!

Mrs. Crewe gave him her place, and he sat by me, and entered into a most animated conversation upon Lord Macartney and his Chinese expedition, and the two Chinese youths who were to accompany it. These last he described minutely, and spoke of the extent of the undertaking in high, and perhaps fanciful, terms, but with allusions and anecdotes intermixed, so full of general information and brilliant ideas, that I soon felt the whole of my first enthusiasm return, and with it a sensation of pleasure that made the day delicious to me.

After this my father joined us, and politics took the lead. He spoke then with an eagerness and a vehemence that instantly banished the graces, though it redoubled the energies, of his discourse. "The French Revolution," he said, "which began by authorising and legalising injustice, and which by rapid steps had proceeded to every species of despotism except owning a despot, was now menacing all the universe and all mankind with the most violent concussion of principle and order." My father heartily joined, and I tacitly assented to his doctrines, though I feared not with his fears.

One speech I must repeat, for it is explanatory of his conduct, and nobly explanatory. When he had expatiated upon the present dangers, even to English liberty and property, from the contagion of havoc and novelty, he earnestly exclaimed, "This it is that has made ME an abettor and supporter of Kings! Kings are necessary, and, if we would preserve peace and prosperity, we must preserve THEM. We must all put our shoulders to the work! Ay, and stoutly, too!"

This subject lasted till dinner.

At dinner Mr. Burke sat next Mrs. Crewe, and I had the happiness to be seated next Mr. Burke; and my other neighbour was his amiable son.

The dinner, and the dessert when the servants were removed, were delightful. How I wish my dear Susanna and Fredy could meet this wonderful man when he is easy, happy, and with people he cordially likes! But politics, even on his own side, must always be excluded; his irritability is so terrible on that theme that it gives immediately to his face the expression of a man who is going to defend himself from murderers.

I can give you only a few little detached traits of what passed, as detail would be endless.

Charles Fox being mentioned, Mrs. Crewe told us that he had lately said, upon being shown some passage in Mr. Burke's book which he had warmly opposed, but which had, in the event, made its own justification, very candidly, "Well! Burke is right— but Burke is often right, only he is right too soon."

"Had Fox seen some things in that book," answered Mr. Burke, "as soon, he would at this moment, in all probability, be first minister of this country."

"What!" cried Mrs. Crewe, "with Pitt?—No!—no!—Pitt won't go out, and Charles Fox will never make a coalition with Pitt."

"And why not?" said Mr. Burke, drily; "why not this coalition as well as other coalitions?"

Nobody tried to answer this.

"Charles Fox, however," said Mr. Burke afterwards, "can never internally like the French Revolution. He is entangled; but, in himself, if he could find no other objection to it, he has at least too much taste for such a revolution."

Mr. Elliot related that he had lately been in a company of some of the first and most distinguished men of the French nation, now fugitives here, and had asked them some questions about the new French ministry; they had answered that they knew them not even by name till now! "Think," he cried, "what a ministry that must be! Suppose a new administration formed here of Englishmen of whom we had never before heard the names! what statesmen they must be! how prepared and fitted for government! To *begin* by being at the helm!"

Mr. Richard Burke related, very comically, various censures cast upon his brother, accusing him of being the friend of despots, and the abettor of slavery, because he had been shocked at the imprisonment of the King of France, and was anxious to preserve our own limited monarchy in the same state in which it so long had flourished.

Mr. Burke looked half alarmed at his brother's opening, but, when he had finished, he very good-humouredly poured out a glass of wine, and, turning to me, said, "Come then—here's slavery for ever!"

This was well understood, and echoed round the table with hearty laughter.

"This would do for you completely, Mr. Burke," said Mrs. Crewe, "if it could get into a newspaper! Mr. Burke, they would say, has now spoken out; the truth has come to light unguardedly, and his real defection from the cause of true liberty is acknowledged. I should like to draw up the paragraph!"

"And add," said Mr. Burke, "the toast was addressed to Miss Burney, in order to pay court to the Queen!"

This sport went on till, upon Mr. Elliot's again mentioning France and the rising Jacobins, Mr. Richard Burke loudly gave a new toast—"Come!" cried he, "here's confusion to confusion!"

Mr. Windham, who has gone into Norfolk for the summer, was frequently mentioned, and always with praise. Mr. Burke, upon Mr. Elliot's saying something of his being very thin, warmly exclaimed, "He is just as he should be! If I were Windham this minute, I should not wish to be thinner, not fatter, nor taller, nor shorter, nor any way, nor in anything, altered."

Some time after, speaking of former days, you may believe I was struck enough to hear Mr. Burke say to Mrs. Crewe, "I wish you had known Mrs. Delany! She was a pattern of a perfect fine lady, a real fine lady, of other days! Her manners were faultless; her deportment was all elegance, her speech was all sweetness, and her air and address all dignity. I always looked up to her as the model of an accomplished woman of former times."

Do you think I heard such a testimony to my beloved departed friend unmoved?

Afterwards, still to Mrs. Crewe, he proceeded to say she had been married to Mr. Wycherley, the author. There I ventured to interrupt him, and tell him I fancied that must be some great mistake, as I had been well acquainted with her history from her own mouth. He seemed to have heard it from some good authority; but I could by no means accede by belief, as her real life and memoirs had been so long in my hands, written by herself to a certain period, and, for some way, continued by me. This, however, I did not mention.

When we left the dining-parlour to the gentlemen, Miss F_____ seized my arm, without the smallest previous speech, and, with a prodigious Irish brogue, said, "Miss Burney, I am so glad you can't think to have this favourable opportunity of making an intimacy with you! I have longed to know you ever since I became rational!"

I was glad, too, that nobody heard her! She made me walk off with her in the garden, whither we had adjourned for a stroll, at a full gallop, leaning upon my arm, and putting her face close to mine, and sputtering at every word from excessive eagerness.

"I have the honour to know some of your relations in Ireland," she continued; "that is, if they an't yours, which they are very sorry for, they are your sister's, which is almost the same thing. Mr. Shirley first lent me 'Cecilia;' and he was so delighted to hear my remarks! Mrs. Shirley's a most beautiful creature; she's grown so large and so big! and all her daughters are beautiful; so is all the family. I never saw Captain Phillips, but I dare say he's beautiful."

She is quite a wild Irish girl.

Presently she talked of Miss Palmer, "O, she loves you!" she cried; "she says she saw you last Sunday, and she never was so happy in her life. She said you looked sadly."

This Miss F_____ is a handsome girl, and seems very good humoured. I imagine her but just imported, and I doubt not but the soft-mannered, and well-bred, and quiet Mrs. Burke will soon subdue this exuberance of loquacity.

I gathered afterwards from Mrs. Crewe, that my curious new acquaintance made innumerable inquiries concerning my employment and office under the Queen. I find many people much disturbed to know whether I had the place of the Duchess of Ancaster, on one side, or of a chambermaid, on the other. Truth is apt to lie between *conjectures.*

The party returned with two very singular additions to its number—Lord Loughborough, and Mr. and Mrs. Erskine. They have villas at Hampstead, and were met in the walk; Mr. Erskine else would not, probably, have desired to meet Mr. Burke, who openly in the House of Commons asked him if he knew what friendship meant, when he pretended to call him, Mr. Burke, his friend?

There was an evident disunion of the cordiality of the party from this time. My father, Mr. Richard Burke, his nephew, and Mr. Elliot entered into some general discourse; Mr. Burke took up a volume of Boileau, and read aloud, though to himself, and with a pleasure that soon made him seem to forget all intruders; Lord Loughborough joined Mrs. Burke; and Mr. Erskine, seating himself next to Mrs. Crewe, engrossed her entirely, yet talked loud enough for all to hear who were not engaged themselves.

For me, I sat next Mrs. Erskine, who seems much a woman of the world, for she spoke with me just as freely, and readily, and easily as if we had been old friends.

Mr. Erskine enumerated all his avocations to Mrs. Crewe, and, amongst others, mentioned, very calmly, having to plead against Mr. Crewe upon a manor business in Cheshire. Mrs.

Crewe hastily and alarmed interrupted him, to inquire what he meant, and what might ensure to Mr. Crewe? "O, nothing but the loss of the lordship upon that spot," he coolly answered; "but I don't know that it will be given against him; I only know I shall have three hundred pounds for it."

Mrs. Crewe looked thoughtful; and Mr. Erskine then began to speak of the new Association for Reform, by the friends of the people, headed by Messrs. Grey and Sheridan, and sustained by Mr. Fox, and openly opposed by Mr. Windham, as well as by Mr. Burke. He said much of the use they had made of his name, though he had never yet been to the society; and I began to understand that he meant to disavow it; but presently he added, "I don't know whether I shall ever attend—I have so much to do—so little time: however, the people must be supported."

"Pray, will you tell me," said Mrs. Crewe, drily, "what you mean by the people? I never knew."

He looked surprised, but evaded any answer, and soon after took his leave, with his wife, who seems by no means to admire him as much as he admires himself, if I may judge by short odd speeches which dropped from her. The eminence of Mr. Erskine seems all for public life; in private, his excessive egotisms undo him.

Lord Loughborough instantly took his seat next to Mrs. Crewe; and presently related a speech which Mr. Erskine has lately made at some public meeting, and which he opened to this effect:—"As for me, gentlemen, I have some title to give my opinions freely. Would you know what my title is derived from? I challenge any man to inquire! If he ask my birth,—its geneal-ogy may dispute with kings! If my wealth, it is all for which I have time to hold out my hand! If my talents,—No! of those, gentle-men, I leave you to judge for yourselves!"

But I have now time for no more upon this day, except that Mr. and Mrs. Burke, in making their exit, gave my father and me the most cordial invitation to Beaconsfield in the course of the summer or autumn. And, indeed, I should delight to accept it.

Mrs. Crewe, my father, and myself spent the evening together, a little in talking politics, when she gave me the pleasure to hear her say Mr. Windham was looked up to by all parties, for his principles as much as for his abilities. We read Rogers's sweet poem on Memory, and some other things, and retired in very serene good humour, I believe, with one another.

Bibliographical Note

Although many editions of Burke's works have been published, none of them is adequately edited; this remains perhaps the chief gap in the scholarly editing of great English authors. The not yet completed Oxford *Writings and Speeches* is surely extensively annotated and it contains the best textual editing, but it has been aptly criticized for an anti-Burkean bias, especially in the volume containing Burke's writings about the French Revolution. Most of the passages quoted in this biography are taken from the text of the Rivington edition (sixteen volumes, London, 1826).

But Burke's letters are readily available in a scholarly edition, Thomas W. Copeland and others, editors, *The Correspondence of Edmund Burke* (ten volumes, Chicago, 1958-1978). Copeland's carefully prepared collection is now recognized as the most important contribution to Burke scholarship this century. There exists the earlier edition of Burke's letters prepared by Earl Fitzwilliam and Sir Richard Bourke (four volumes, London, 1844).

As for manuscripts, the majority of these are now available for public inspection at the Sheffield Central Library—including those from the Rockingham and Fitzwilliam papers formerly at Wentworth Woodhouse. The second largest collection is held by the Northampton-shire Record Society, at Lamport Hall—formerly in the Fitzwilliam papers at Milton. Lesser collections are scattered across Britain and America.

A Bibliography of Edmund Burke, compiled by William B. Todd, was published by Rupert Hart-Davies, London, 1964. *Edmund Burke: A Bibliography of Secondary Studies to 1982,* prepared by Clara I. Gandy and Peter J. Stanlis (New York: Garland, 1983) is a thorough piece of work, with a valuable essay, "Burke's Historical Reputation: 1797-1981," by Stanlis.

Most of the more important biographies and specialized studies of Burke have been cited in the preceding footnotes and chapter-notes. Some not cited, but still of value either for information or for criticism, are the following:

Ayling, Stanley, *Edmund Burke: His Life and Opinions* (New York: St. Martin's, 1988).

Baumann, A. A., *Burke: The Founder of Conservatism* (London, 1929).

Bisset, Robert, *The Life of Edmund Burke* (London, 1798).

Blakemore, Stephen, *Burke and the Fall of Language: The French Revolution as a Linguistic Event* (Hanover, N.H.: University of New England Press, 1988).

Blakemore, Stephen, ed., *Burke and the French Revolution: Bicentennial Essays* (Athens: University of Georgia Press, 1992).

Burke, Peter, *The Public and Domestic Life of the Right Hon. Edmund Burke* (London, 1854).

Burke, Peter, *The Wisdom and Genius of the Right Hon. Edmund Burke* (London, 1845).

Canavan, Francis, *Edmund Burke: Providence and Prescription* (Durham, N.C.: Carolina University Press, 1987).

Canavan, Francis, *The Political Economy of Edmund Burke: The Role of Property in His Thought* (New York: Fordham University Press, 1995).

Chapman, Gerald W., *Edmund Burke: The Practical Imagination* (Cambridge, Mass., 1967).

Croly, George, A *Memoir of the Political Life of the Right Honourable Edmund Burke* (2 vols., Edinburgh, 1840).

Crowe, Ian, ed., *The Enduring Edmund Burke: Bicentennial Essays* (Intercollegiate Studies Institute, 1997).

Fennessey, R. R., *Burke, Paine, and the Rights of Man: a Difference of Political Opinion* (The Hague, 1963).

Freeman, Michael, *Edmund Burke and the Critique of Political Radicalism* (Chicago: University of Chicago Press, 1980).

Frohnen, Bruce, *Virtue and the Promise of Conservatism: The Legacy of Burke and Tocqueville* (University Press of Kansas, 1993).

Hampsher-Monk, Iain, *The Political Philosophy of Edmund Burke* (New York: Longman, 1987).

Hoffman, Ross J. S., *The Marquis: A Study of Lord Rockingham, 1739-1785* (New York, 1978).

Langford, Paul, ed., *Edmund Burke, Works,* Vols. 2, 3, 5, 6, 8, 9 (Oxford: Clarendon Press, 1981-96).

Macknight, Thomas, *History of the Life and Times of Edmund Burke* (3 vols., London, 1856-1860).

Magnus, Sir Philip, *Edmund Burke: A Life* (London, 1939).

Morley, John, *Edmund Burke: A Historical Study* (London, 1879).

Murray, Robert H., *Edmund Burke* (Oxford, 1931).

Noonan, John T., Chapter Fourteen, *Bribes* (New York: MacMillan, 1984). This is an excellent treatment of the legal aspects of the Hastings impeachment.

O'Brien, Conor Cruise, *The Great Melody* (Chicago: University of Chicago Press, 1992).

O'Gorman, Frank, *Edmund Burke: His Political Philosophy* (Bloomington: Indiana University Press, 1973).

Pappin III, Joseph, *The Metaphysics of Edmund Burke* (New York: Fordham University Press, 1992).

Reynolds, E. E., *Edmund Burke: Christian Statesman* (London, 1948).

Ritchie, Daniel, ed., *Further Reflections on the Revolution in France* (Indianapolis: Liberty Press, 1992).

Ritchie, Daniel, ed., *Edmund Burke: Appraisals and Applications* (Rutgers, N.J.: Transaction Publishers, 1990).

Robertson, J. B., *Lectures on the Life, Writings, and Times, of Edmund Burke* (London, 1868).

Stanlis, Peter J., *Edmund Burke: The Enlightenment and Revolution* (New Brunswick, N.J.: Transaction Press, 1991).

Stanlis, Peter J., *Edmund Burke and the Natural Law* (Shreveport, LA: Huntington House, 1986).

Valentine, Alan, *Lord North,* (2 vols., Norman, Okla., 1967).

Welsh, Jennifer M., *Edmund Burke and International Relations: The Commonwealth of Europe and the Crusade against the French Revolution* (Oxford: St. Martin's Press, 1995).

Frederick G. Whelan, *Edmund Burke and India: Political Morality and Empire* (Pittsburgh: University of Pittsburgh Press, 1996).

There exist too many critical essays—as distinguished from books—and unpublished doctoral dissertations about Burke for any listing to be undertaken here.

References to Burke in the memoirs and diaries of the period naturally are abundant. Here one may recommend particularly—in addition to such books cited in the preceding notes—the numerous volumes of *The Private Papers of James Boswell;* Boswell's *Life of Samuel Johnson; The Life of George Crabbe, by his Son; The Early Life and Diaries of William Windham* (edited by R. W. Ketton-Cremer); *The Windham Papers; The Jenkinson Papers, 1760-1766;* Horace Walpole's *Memoirs of the Reign of George the Third* (and also Walpole's letters, of course); *Memoirs of the Marquis of Rockingham; The Life and Times of Henry Grattan; The Verney Papers; Correspondence of the Earl of Chatham.*

For the general history of the time, the great work is W. E. H. Lecky's *History of England in the Eighteenth Century.* See also his *History of Ireland in the Eighteenth Century,* and his *Leaders of Public Opinion in Ireland.* For the thought of the age, see particularly Leslie Stephen's *History of English Thought in the Eighteenth Century,* and his *English Literature and Society in the Eighteenth Century;* also Ernst Cassirer, *The Philosophy of the Enlightenment.*

The studies of the Old Regime and the Revolution in France by Taine and by Tocqueville remain very valuable. See also Franz Funck-Brentano's *The Old Regime in France.*

Gouverneur Morris' *Diary of the French Revolution* offers an American's view.

For a good account of the remnant of the Mughul Empire in Hastings' time and later, see Percival Spear, *Twilight of the Mughuls: Studies in Late Mughul Delhi.*

Volumes VII, VIII, and IX of *The New Cambridge Modern History* cover Burke's period competently. *The Dictionary of National Biography* contains accounts of nearly everyone mentioned in this book.

For quite different reasons, these three works also are worth consulting: Sir William Holdsworth, *A History of English Law,* Vols. XI and XIII (the period of Burke and Bentham); M. Dorothy George's *English Political Caricature: A Study of Opinion and Propaganda,* Vol. 1; and Nicholas K. Robinson's *Edmund Burke: A Life in Caricature.*

This writer's book, *The Conservative Mind* : *From Burke to Eliot* contains (chapter two) a more detailed and coherent examination of Burke's political philosophy than can be contrived within the limits of the present volume, which is intended to be chiefly biographical.

Notes

CHAPTER 1

1. Edmund Burke, *Letter to a Noble Lord,* edited by W. Murison (Cambridge, 1920), p. 138.

2. John Morley, *Burke* (English Men of Letters Series, London, 1888), p. 315.

3. Paul Elmer More, *Aristocracy and Justice* (Shelburne Essays, Vol. IX, Boston, 1915), p. 3.

4. William Butler Yeats, "Stories of Red Hanrahan," in *Mythologies* (London, 1958), p. 215.

5. Mary Leadbeater (editor), *The Leadbeater Papers* (2 vols., London, 1862), Vol. I, pp. 49-51.

6. The most thorough account of these years is in Arthur P. I. Samuels, *The Early Life, Correspondence, and Writings of the Rt. Hon. Edmund Burke, LL.D.* (Cambridge, 1923).

7. *The Correspondence of Edmund Burke* (edited by Thomas W. Copeland, Chicago, 1958), Vol. I, p. 74.

8. See the admirable edition, with introduction and notes, by J. T. Boulton (London, 1958).

9. See "Several Scattered Hints concerning Philosophy and Learning," in *A Note-Book of Edmund Burke* (edited by H. V. F. Somerset, Cambridge, 1957), pp. 82-83.

10. "Miscellaneous Essays," *The Annual Register, 1760*; mentioned in Somerset, *Note-Book, op. cit.,* p. 13.

11. *Correspondence of Burke, op. cit.,* I, p. 101.

12. See the able study of Burke's juridical views by Peter Stanlis, *Edmund Burke and the Natural Law* (Ann Arbor, 1958).

13. "The Character of _____ [Mrs. Edmund Burke]," in Somerset, *Note-Book, op. cit.,* pp. 52-54.

CHAPTER 2

1. H. J. C. Grierson, "Edmund Burke," in *The Cambridge History of English Literature* (Cambridge, 1932), Vol. XI, pp. 3-4.

2. J. T. Boulton (editor), Burke's *Philosophical Enquiry into the Origin of Our Ideas of the Sublime and Beautiful* (London, 1958), p. lxxvi.

3. For Burke's dissent from the dominant climate of opinion in the eighteenth century, see Louis I. Bredvold, *The Brave New World of the Enlightenment* (Ann Arbor, 1961), pp. 125-148; also Alfred Cobban, *Edmund Burke and the Revolt against the Eighteenth Century* (London, 1929).

4. Harvey Wish, *The American Historian* (New York, 1960), p. 40.

5. For a hostile examination of the Burkes' finances and speculative ventures, consult Dixon Wecter, *Edmund Burke and his Kinsmen: A Study of the Statesman's Financial*

Integrity and Private Relationships (Boulder, Colorado, 1939).

6. See Walter D. Love, "Burke's Transition from a Literary to a Political Career," in *The Burke Newsletter,* No. 22, winter, 1964-65.

7. *Correspondence of Burke,* I, *op. cit.,* p. 169.

8. Love, *op. cit.,* pp. 387-388.

9. For a thorough treatment of this large subject, see Walter D. Mahoney, *Edmund Burke and Ireland* (Cambridge, Massachusetts, 1960).

10. Burke to O'Hara, 23 December, 1766 *(Correspondence of Burke,* I, *op. cit.,* p. 285).

11. For remarks on the Whigs of Burke's time, see Lord David Cecil, *The Young Melbourne* (London, 1939), p. 20; and Sir Philip Magnus, *Edmund Burke: A Prophet of the Eighteenth Century* (London, 1939), pp. 23-24.

12. Bertram Newman, *Edmund Burke* (London, 1927), p. 37.

13. *Correspondence of Burke,* I, *op. cit.,* p. 211.

14. *Ibid.,* p. 223.

15. Burke to O'Hara, 11 December, 1767, *ibid.,* p. 340.

CHAPTER 3

1. Carl B. Cone, *Burke and the Nature of Politics: The Age of the American Revolution* (Lexington, Kentucky, 1957), Vol. 1, p. 69.

2. For a thorough account of these controversies, see John C. Miller, *Origins of the American Revolution* (Boston, 1943); and H. Trevor Colbourn, *The Lamp of Experience:*

Whig History and the Intellectual Origins of the American Revolution (Chapel Hill, 1965). The principal speeches in the controversy, on either side of the Atlantic, are conveniently collected by Max Beloff in *The Debate on the American Revolution, 1761-1783* (London, 1949).

3. The best summary of Burke on American affairs is in Ross J. S. Hoffman's *Edmund Burke, New York Agent, with his Letters to the New York Assembly and Intimate Correspondence with Charles O'Hara, 1761-1766* (Philadelphia, 1956).

4. Although Burke was consistently opposed to the slave trade and slavery, he has been injudiciously criticized by some writers for not approving the emancipation of slaves during the American Revolution. (See, for instance, Martin Kallich, "Some British Opinions of the American Revolution," *Burke Newsletter,* No. 12, summer, 1962.) Here Burke's argument was rather like his denunciation of the employment of savage Indian auxiliaries against the colonists: social order would be destroyed, and "total" war sanctioned, without any provision for the welfare of the freedmen; besides, this tactic was a two-edged sword, and Negro slaves might choose to aid the rebels, rather than their dubiously-sincere "emancipators."

5. John Morley, *Burke* (English Men of Letters Series) (London, 1888), p. 116.

6. For Burke's financial perplexities and other damage to Burke's reputation, see Thomas W. Copeland's essay, "The Little Dogs and All," in his *Our Eminent Friend Edmund Burke: Six Essays* (New Haven, 1949). For the affair of the East India stocks, see Lucy S. Sutherland and John A. Woods, *The East India Speculations of William Burke* (Proceedings of the Leeds Philosophical and Literary

Society: Literary and Historical Section, Vol. XI, Part VII, January, 1966, pp. 183-216). Sutherland and Woods show that Edmund Burke was not a principal in the speculation.

7. See G. E. Weare, *Edmund Burke's Connection with Bristol: From 1774 till 1780* (Bristol, 1894).

8. For Lord North, see, for instance, Herbert Butterfield, *George III, Lord North, and the People: 1779-1780* (London, 1949).

9. O'Hara to Burke, 11 July, 1771, in Hoffman, *Burke, New York Agent,* p. 493.

10. Hoffman, *op. cit.,* p. 121.

11. Hans Barth, *The Idea of Order: Contributions to a Philosophy of Politics* (Dordrecht, 1960), Chapter II.

12. Hoffman, *op. cit.,* p. 181.

CHAPTER 4

1. Peter Stanlis, "Edmund Burke in the Twentieth Century," in *The Relevance of Edmund Burke,* ed. by Stanlis (New York, 1964), pp. 24-25.

2. Ross J. S. Hoffman, "Edmund Burke as a Practical Politician," in Stanlis, *Relevance of Burke,* pp. 115-116.

3. *Ibid.,* p. 111.

4. For a sample of the views of Namier's disciples, see the article on Edmund Burke by John Brooke, in Namier and Brooke, *The History of Parliament: The House of Commons, 1754-1790,* Vol. II (London, 1965). For a more measured assessment, see Herbert Butterfield, *George III, Lord North, and the People: 1779-1780* (London, 1949); also his *George III and the Historians.*

5. Harvey C. Mansfield, Jr., *Statesmanship and Party Government: A Study of Burke and Bolingbroke* (Chicago, 1965), p. 17.

6. Jeffrey Hart, *Viscount Bolingbroke, Tory Humanist* (London, 1965), pp. 93-94.

7. For a penetrating comparison of the rhetoric of Burke with the rhetoric of Paine, see James T. Boulton, *The Language of Politics in the Age of Wilkes and Burke* (London, 1963).

8. See Hart, *op. cit.,* pp. 149-150.

9. For comments on such passages in the *Discontents,* see the most scholarly edition—that of E. J. Payne, *Edmund Burke: Select Works,* Vol. I (Oxford, 1904). Jeffrey Hart's edition (Chicago, 1964) has a good introduction.

10. Newman, *op. cit.,* pp. 127-128.

11. Ross J. S. Hoffman and Paul Levack, *Burke's Politics* (New York, 1949), p. 213.

12. Francis Canavan, "Burke as a Reformer," in Stanlis, *The Relevance of Edmund Burke,* pp. 105-106.

13. Carl B. Cone, *Burke and the Nature of Politics* (Vol II): *The Age of the French Revolution* (Lexington, Kentucky, 1964), p. 90.

CHAPTER 5

1. See Sophia Weitzman, *Warren Hastings and Philip Francis* (Manchester, 1929).

2. *Correspondence of Edmund Burke,* Vol. IV, July, 1778-June, 1782 (edited by John A. Woods), p. 447.

3. William Burke to Richard Burke the younger, Decem-

ber 30, 1785, in the Chatham Papers, G.D. 8/118, Public Record Office, London. For an amusing account of Will Burke's eccentric behavior in Madras at this time, see *Memoirs of William Hickey* (edited by Alfred Spencer, fifth edition, London, 1948), Vol. III.

4. *Correspondence of Edmund Burke,* Vol. V, July, 1782-June, 1789 (edited by Holden Furber), pp. 241-243.

5. Cone, *Burke and the Nature of Politics,* II, pp. 114-115.

6. Keith Feiling, *Warren Hastings* (London, 1954), p. 369.

7. See Russell Kirk's article "Natural Law" in *The Dictionary of Historical Terms* (edited by Joseph Dunner, New York, 1967).

8. Peter Stanlis, *Edmund Burke and the Natural* Law, pp. 88-89.

9. Francis Canavan, *The Political Reason of Edmund Burke,* p. 92. See also Gaetano L. Vincitorio, *Edmund Burke's International Politics* (Fordham University doctoral dissertation, 1950, as yet unpublished), Chapter V, "British Imperialism in India."

10. Cone, *op. cit.,* II, pp. 96, 105, 121, 188-189, 190-191, 207, 254-256.

11. Bertram Newman, *Edmund Burke,* pp. 228-229.

12. *The Epistolary Correspondence of the Right Hon. Edmund Burke and Dr. French Laurence* (London, 1827), pp. 53-56.

CHAPTER 6

1. Burke to Fitzwilliam, November 29, 1793, in Wentworth Woodhouse Papers, Book I, p. 945 (Sheffield

Central Library).

2. Jean François de La Harpe's *Prophétie de Cazotte,* as paraphrased by Hippolyte Taine in the concluding chapter of *The Ancient Regime* (translated by John Durant, New York, 1881). See also C. A. Sainte-Beuve, *Causeries du Lundi,* Vol. V.

3. Herbert Hoover identified the apocalyptic "Fourth Horseman" as personified Revolution. See Herbert Hoover, with Marie Therese Nichols, "Myth of the Fourth Horseman," *The Saturday Review,* September 30, 1958, pp. 17 ff.

4. Augustine Birrell, *Obiter Dicta,* Second Series (London, 1894), pp. 172-174.

5. Burke to John Bourke, November, 1777, in *The Correspondence of Edmund Burke,* Vol. III, July 1774-June 1778 (edited by George H. Guttridge), p. 403.

6. Ross J. S. Hoffman, "Tocqueville and Burke," in *The Burke Newsletter,* II, No. 4 (spring-summer, 1961), p. 46.

7. Burke to Richard Shackleton, September 5, 1770, in *Correspondence of Edmund Burke,* Vol. 11, July 1768-June 1774 (edited by Lucy S. Sutherland), p. 150.

8. Only six should be executed, Burke asked—though those on separate days, and in conspicuous places. Although the government was not quite so forgiving, no more than twenty-six criminal rioters were put to death.

9. See Basil O'Connel, "Richard Burke and James Cotter, Jr.," in *The Burke Newsletter,* VI, No. I (fall, 1964), pp. 360-362.

10. See Maurice James Craig, *The Volunteer Earl: Being the Life and Times of James Caulfield, First Earl of Charlemont* (London, 1948).

11. See the analysis of this *Letter* by Thomas H. D. Mahoney, *Edmund Burke and Ireland,* Chapter VI. This

and Burke's other principal writings and speeches on Ireland were collected into one volume by Matthew Arnold, *Edmund Burke and Irish Affairs* (London, 1881). For the general subject, see also William O'Brien, *Edmund Burke as an Irishman* (second edition, Dublin, 1926).

12. Hoffman and Levack, *Burke's Politics,* p. 510.

13. Mahoney, *Edmund Burke and Ireland,* pp. 316-323.

CHAPTER 7

1. Henry Crabb Robinson, in 1811, re-read Burke's speeches during the Regency debate. "Their extravagance and intemperance is not less than their splendour.... In one of his vehement bursts, after representing the King as hurled from his throne by God, he asserted that the assigning him an establishment was covering his bed with purple, putting a reed in his hand and crown of thorns on his brow, and crying: Hail King of the British! The seeming scorn of such an allusion, as on other occasions, raised a hostility to the orator quite incompatible with the desired effect of eloquence, to propitiate; yet abstracted from such an impression the image is very happy. Charles Lamb, however, said it was in a vile taste, a little in Mr. Fuller's style." *Henry Crabb Robinson on Books and Their Writers,* edited by Edith J. Morley (London, 1938), Vol. 1, p. 20.

2. Woodrow Wilson, "Edmund Burke and the French Revolution," *The Century Magazine,* Vol. LXII (N.S., XL), September, 1901, p. 784.

3. Paine certainly wrote one letter to Burke during this period, and perhaps others; also he may have conversed

with him in the autumn of 1789. See Copeland, *Our Eminent Friend Edmund Burke,* Chapter V, "Burke, Paine, and Jefferson."

4. Lord Percy of Newcastle, *The Heresy of Democracy: A Study in the History of Government* (London, 1954), p. 188.

5. For a criticism of the rationalistic politics which emerged in the French Revolution and which have exerted considerable power ever since, see Michael Oakeshott, *Rationalism in Politics: And Other Essays* (London, 1962).

6. Wilson, *op. cit.,* p. 792.

7. Many editions of the *Reflections* exist; that best annotated, the second volume of E. J. Payne's *Burke: Select Works* (Oxford, 1898), unhappily is long out of print. The present writer's introduction appears in the edition of the *Reflections* published by Arlington House (New Rochelle, New York, 1965).

8. This war of pamphlets may be surveyed by consulting two convenient anthologies: Alfred Cobban (editor), *The Debate on the French Revolution, 1789-1799* (London, 1950), and Ray B. Browne (editor), *The Burke-Paine Controversy: Texts and Criticism* (New York, 1963). The latter volume contains comments by twentieth-century writers.

9. For two brief studies of Burke's influence on American men of politics, see James P. McClellan, "Judge Story's Debt to Burke," in *The Burke Newsletter,* Vol. VII, No. 3 (spring, 1966), pp. 583-586; and Russell Kirk, "John Randolph of Roanoke on the Genius of Edmund Burke," *The Burke Newsletter,* Vol. IV, No. I (fall, 1962), pp. 167-169. For some general remarks on Burke's meaning for Americans, see Russell Kirk's review of the second edition of Clinton Rossiter's *Conservatism in America,* in *The Burke*

Newsletter, Vol. IV, No. 2 (winter, 1962-63), pp. 190-193.

10. Walter Scott to Henry Francis Scott the younger, of Harden, January 10, 1831, in John Lockhart, *Memoirs of the Life of Sir Walter Scott, Bart.* (Edinburgh, 1853), Vol. X, p. 32.

11. James T. Boulton, *The Language of Politics in the Age of Wilkes and Burke,* Chapter VIII.

12. *Ibid.,* p. 149.

13. See Russell Kirk, "Edmund Burke and Natural Rights," in *The Review of Politics,* Vol. 13, No. 4 (October, 1951), pp. 441-456; also Kirk, "Burke and the Philosophy of Prescription," *Journal of the History of Ideas,* Vol. XIV, No. 3 (June, 1953), pp. 365-389.

14. Boulton, *op. cit.,* pp. 260-261.

15. Burke to Fitzwilliam, November 29, 1793, in Wentworth Woodhouse Papers, Book I, p. 945 (Sheffield Central Library).

16. Louis Bredvold, *The Brave New World of the Enlightenment,* p. 134.

17. For Burke's influence on Wordsworth, Coleridge, and others, see Edward Dowden, *The French Revolution and English Literature* (London, 1897); also Basil Willey, *The Eighteenth Century Background* (London, 1949). For Burke's association with literary people of his own generation, see the thorough study by Donald Cross Bryant, *Edmund Burke and his Literary Friends* (St. Louis, 1939).

CHAPTER 8

1. John MacCunn, *The Political Philosophy of Burke* (London, 1913), pp. 130-131.

2. Charles Parkin, *The Moral Basis of Burke's Political Thought* (Cambridge, 1956), pp. 87-88, 95-96, 107-108.

3. Burke to Francis, February 12, 1790, in *The Francis Letters: Sir Philip Francis and Other Members of the Family,* edited by Beata Francis and Eliza Keary (2 vols., London, n.d.), Vol. II, pp. 380-386.

4. Walpole to Miss Mary Berry, May 12, 1791, in *A Selection of the Letters of Horace Walpole,* edited by W. S. Lewis (New York, 1926), p. 443.

5. Sir James Mackintosh, *Memoirs of the Life of the Right Honourable Sir James Mackintosh,* edited by Robert James Mackintosh (2 vols., London, 1836), Vol. I, pp. 128-129.

6. Burke to Richard Burke, September 26, 1791, in Fitzwilliam and Bourke, *Correspondence of Burke,* III, pp. 341-351.

7. Leo Strauss, *Natural Right and History* (Chicago, 1953), p. 318, and the latter half of Chapter VI. See also Richard Weaver, *The Ethics of Rhetoric* (Chicago, 1953), Chapter III.

8. N. W. Wraxall, *Posthumous Memoirs of His Own Time* (3 vols., London, 1836), Vol. III, p. 344.

CHAPTER 9

1. "Burke thought Pitt had great parts but a little soul,— none of his Father's characteristic grasp of mind." Joseph Farington, July 19, 1797, in *The Farington Diary* (2 vols., London, 1923), Vol. 1, p. 212.

2. See C. P. Ives, "The Gregories Today," in *The Burke Newsletter,* Vol. IV, No. 2 (winter, 1962-63), pp. 188-189.

3. *Henry Crabb Robinson on Books and Their Writers,* Vol. II, p. 777.

4. *(Mémoires d'outre tombe) The Memoirs of François René, Vicomte de Chateaubriand,* translated by Alexander Teixeira de Mattos (5 vols., London, 1902), Vol. II, pp. 144-145.

5. *Memoirs of the Life of Sir James Mackintosh,* X, pp. 91-92.

6. See Keith Grahame Feiling, *The Second Tory Party:* 1714-1832 (London, 1951), Chapter XIII.

7. E. J. Payne (editor), *Burke: Select Works: Four Letters on the Proposals for Peace with the Regicide Directory of France* (Oxford, 1878), p. xl.

8. Fitzwilliam and Bourke, *Correspondence of Burke,* IV, pp. 131-136.

9. James Prior, *Memoir of the Life and Character of the Right Hon. Edmund Burke* (London, 1824), p. 447.

10. *Diary and Letters of Madame D'Arblay* (7 vols., London, 1854), Vol. VI, p. 98.

11. Sir Charles Petrie, *George Canning* (London, 1930), p. 23.

12. Feiling, *op. cit.,* p. 329.

13. Yeats, "The Seven Sages," in *The Collected Poems of W. B. Yeats* (London, 1952), p. 272.

14. Burke's "common soldier" is Arnold of Winkelried, the Swiss who broke in upon the spears at Sempach; his child is Hannibal, taking at the age of twelve his oath to make undying war upon Rome; his girl at the inn is Joan of Arc.

Index

A

B

C

R

S

X

Y